The Stolen Presidency

AN UNPRECEDENTED AFRICAN POLITICAL TRAGEDY

Jamiu Abiola

In memory of my father and my mother, Moshood and Kudirat Abiola, and all the other people who were killed during the battle to retrieve the stolen presidency.

Author's Note

In November, 1998, I was sitting in the airport in Abuja, Nigeria where I was forced to wait for more than four hours after bad weather had caused a delay in my flight to Lagos. Once the announcement of the delay was made, the view before me became chaotic as passengers rained curses at the airline officials in a scene that has become so Nigerian because of the country's very high record of delayed flights. It was right there in the midst of all the disarray that I witnessed what I had never thought would happen after the death of my father, Moshood Abiola, just four months prior to that day.

Five people were divided into two groups. They were involved in a heated debate over whether my father, a man who had sacrificed his life and a huge financial fortune for democracy in Nigeria, deserved to be called a hero or not. I sat quietly, wondering whether the scene in front of me was real, after all my father had won Nigeria's presidential elections and the whole country knew it. He had also died in his battle against the military that had annulled his victory and everyone knew it. Prior to his death, some had criticized him for different reasons, which was a normal thing because no one can be liked by everyone, but I had never expected that such criticism would follow him to his grave after he had become a martyr.

Both sides were very aggressive. One group called him a messiah. The other group labeled him a self-serving businessman. The debate had begun when the leader of what I would later term as 'the pro Abiola group', a stout man with a bald head and a long mustache, declared firmly, "If I am to be honest with you guys, I am not looking forward to the military transition to civilian rule planned by our military president, Abdulsalam, because there would be no Moshood Abiola at the end of the process. He has died and taken our dreams away with him."

He had barely finished his sentence when a tall pregnant woman with long hair and bulky eyes, shouted at him, "Do you really believe that a transition that would have produced Moshood Abiola is what we need? Is that what you really think?" Her tone was firm and laced with sarcasm.

The man looked alarmed. It was as if she had uttered something blasphemous. She did not give him a chance to reply before she continued."My brother, open your eyes and you will see that the purpose of this transition is to find somebody who is the opposite of Moshood Abiola. Somebody who did not get rich through shady government contracts."

Another man interrupted her. Despite his tiny voice, he supported her opinion aggressively. "She is right. She has said it all. All that man wanted was personal glory. He had become famous and rich so the presidency was next. What an insatiable man!"

The pregnant woman smiled. She looked astonished, as if she had not expected his support, and became less aggressive. After a few seconds she stared at the man who had spoken well of my father and gently added, "It is as if you have forgotten the telephone scam that a popular Yoruba singer sang about. What is his name again?" She paused then proceeded. "His name is Fela and he sang of how Moshood Abiola was paid millions of dollars by the Nigerian government to supply telephone lines but he did not execute the contract. Why will such a man ever dream of ruling Nigeria?"

Another man with long afro hair and very thick glasses, who had been quiet all along, stood up. He looked as if he was about to attack the woman, moving very close to her before speaking. "If you are an educated woman then shame on you! Why would you make such weighty allegations against a man who died fighting for a mandate that he received from Nigerians?" He paused, breathing heavily as if he was running out of breath."You consider the words of Fela as facts, the words of a man who was known to sing and dance almost naked on stage. Did Fela ever present any evidence against your elected president? Did he even reveal the source of his information?"

The others begged him to calm down but their attempts were in vain. The duel continued as he launched a verbal assault. "In that case, if Fela says that the baby in your stomach belongs to your husband's best friend without showing any proof, I will believe him right away so that you know how it feels like to be a victim of false accusations."

At that point the others got upset with him and the woman looked as if she was about to cry. The man who spoke first intervened. "Don't be offended, my sister, but on a more serious note, if Moshood Abiola was guilty, as you said, then the two military presidents, General Babangida who annulled his electoral victory and General Abacha who locked him up for claiming it, would have exposed the facts. After all they needed justification for the injustice they had done to him." His eyes were boring on her.

The woman seemed rattled, confused, as if she was about to change her mind about my father. At this point I could take no more. I stood up and left because I no longer cared about their discussion. I walked away from them, wishing that I had never witnessed that debate, to the far end of the airport. I was roaming around aimlessly, thinking about that scene which now seemed like something that had played out in a nightmare. I hoped that I would calm down but my heart refused to stop beating fast.

I looked out of a window, after almost an hour, and saw the sun shining brightly as people walked hurriedly toward the airport's entrance, carrying heavy boxes and suitcases. That was when it dawned on me that I should write a book about my father. From that day I became obsessed with the idea but more than a decade passed before I took one single step. Like many people I am afraid of opening old wounds and remained scared until the summer of 2014.

My children convinced me on that year to take them on a trip to Egypt and within four days, after our arrival, we had gone everywhere from the Pyramids to all the major malls. We began spending more time in the hotel because there was nothing more to do during the remaining five days of our trip. Our vacation suddenly became dull. That was when my eldest child Moshood, out of boredom, asked me about my father. "Tell me everything about my grandfather!" He sounded very serious.

You are in big trouble, I told myself. It was times like this that I regretted naming him after my father because, for some reason, the twelve year old boy felt that being his grandfather's namesake gave him the right to know everything about him. He wanted to walk like him, talk like him and had even joked several times that he would someday become a billionaire like him.

"Me too! I want to know everything about him." added his younger eleven year old sister, whom I had also named after my mother. She sat right next to me, her eyes sparkling with curiosity.

"What exactly do you guys want to know? You can't just say that you want to know everything." My voice was as low as a whisper, a reflection of my strong reluctance to talk about my father.

My wife, Khadija, scolded me at once. "Since when did children know exactly what they want to know or do? Just tell them what you want them to know!"

"But this is not a regular story, it is a tragedy, and vacations are not the right times for children to listen to tragedies." I was still very hesitant but shifted grounds when I realized that I was alone against the rest of them, excluding my youngest son, who seemed very indifferent. "I give up but let me take a short nap first." I stood up and headed toward my room."But no one should blame me if any of you ends up crying or depressed."

I returned after an hour with an initial plan of focusing on my father's life in his forties. This, to me, was the best period in his life but I changed my mind and narrated the darker side of his life, covering the tragedy that turned him and my mother into martyrs. But my first statement sparked a minor disagreement between me and Moshood. "Your grandfather was a president."

"But if he was, why didn't he rule?" replied Moshood with a confident tone and a rebellious look on his face.

I smiled before asking."What is your name and how old are you?"

"Moshood, of course, and I am twelve years old." He was smiling while his younger sister was laughing.

I paused before answering."That is my exact point. Your name is Moshood and you are twelve years old, which is the truth and nothing else matters as long as you know that. The fact that you are a president does not mean that you must rule because your presidency, just like any-thing else, can be stolen from you. That is why history is full of legitimate kings who died in exile because people remain who and what they are even if their positions and titles are stolen from them."

My son was deeply confused, I could tell, but he nodded his head all the same as I continued. I knew he would understand my point by the end of the story which I had surprisingly become eager to narrate. That was how I overcame the phobia about writing this book until I eventually completed it.

Chapter One

July 3, 1996

I WAS RIGHT ALL ALONG. I knew this was going to happen from the very beginning..

I had just returned to Nigeria thirty-nine days after my mother, Kudirat Abiola, the senior wife of my father Moshood Abiola, had been assassinated. My mother's death occurred less than three years after my father's historical victory in a Nigerian presidential election judged by foreign observers as the freest and fairest in the country's history. Yet he had been in jail following his arrest almost two years before my mother's murder. He had declared himself the Nigerian president, a treasonable offense according to the ruling military junta, after failing to convince the country's military ruler General Sani Abacha to hand over power to him as the legitimate president of Nigeria.

I was not alone on this trip to Nigeria, for my immediate elder brother Lekan was with me. By the way, my name is Jamiu Abiola. That day the dilapidated international airport in Lagos and its extreme heat mirrored my gloomy state of mind as I emerged from the plane. But things got worse at the immigration desk where I encountered an officer who, at one glance at my passport, recognized me and condoled me before asking for money. I was baffled at his insensitivity and remained motionless for a few seconds before putting my hand into my pocket and bringing out a twenty dollar bill. The man, showing no signs of shame, grabbed the money as if it was part of an overdue entitlement then gave me my passport after stamping it. I was relieved when I finally walked out of the airport after some additional security checks.

On the drive back home I recalled the day my father announced his presidential ambition to me and my brother. That day, just like now, I was in a car with Lekan but instead of leaving an airport, we were heading towards one. My father had just come to the United States, something he did often, but he also wanted to leave that same day, which was unusual. "I must be in London within the next eleven hours because something has just come up." But he had an urgent announcement to make. "Why don't you drive me to the airport?" He asked my brother before adding, looking at the both of us. 'We will talk on the way because I have an important announcement to make. I would also like to show both of you my new plane." His tone was very jovial.

My brother and I sprang up and, in less than five minutes, we were in the front seat of my brother's car. We had put my father's suitcase inside the boot while he had sat on the back seat. From the rear view mirror I could see his broad smile and wondered whether he was excited by our presence or by the fact that he had just acquired a new plane.

No one spoke for the first five minutes of our one-hour journey to Dulles Airport from Washington D.C. until my father broke the silence. "I am joining the presidential race and, unlike before, this is not a wild goose chase. General Babangida is serious about leaving power this time... This time the coast is very clear."

Despite his upbeat tone he sounded as if he was trying to sell himself an idea, he sounded as if he was trying to convince himself about what he was saying. My reaction was immediate, for I have always had the propensity for being blunt. "Sir, I doubt that General Babangida will hand over power... I really doubt it because power is something that no one wants to give away."

I have never been able to figure out how I made that statement, for I have always been shy around him. But I was remorseful, even before his response, because it was an insensitive thing to say to someone who had been in such high spirits. "What do you know about power? Your knowledge of it, and of politics, is limited because you are still a child. Maybe if I were your age, I would have made such a careless remark." His tone was bitter and he was stammering, which has always been a sign of his anger.

I did not know how to respond and, out of fear of making a bad situation worse, I did not think that I should. But I felt the need to say something. "On a second thought, sir, since General Babangida has been in power for so long, he might be tired of it by now. He might indeed be willing to hand over power to someone else." I uttered those words timidly but they sounded clumsy and compounded my guilt. After the long ensuing silence I wished that the ground would crack open and swallow me up.

My father was quiet for the rest of the journey until we arrived at the airport when he spoke in reference to the Nigerian military president who later annulled his presidential electoral victory, "All I know is that nothing will help Babangida enter heaven, not money and not power. Now let's walk to my new plane so that you can both tell me what you think of it."

My thoughts returned to the present as the car pulled into our expansive family house in Lagos, a white house divided into five sections (each with at least five bedrooms), one section for each of my father's four official wives and an additional section for him where he had an office and received a minimum of five hundred guests daily over a span of twenty years. The house, though the same, wore a sharply different look, for it had now been abandoned. There was no longer a large crowd of desperate people waiting outside its gates, a crowd including the needy and the wealthy. A former Nigerian ruler had once been part of that crowd, which cost one of our security personnel his job, because that particular personnel ought to have granted the former ruler swift entry instead of asking him to fill a form stating his name and purpose of visit. Once again, as I alighted from the car, I wished that my father had taken my warning seriously.

But he was still alive, I reminded myself, even though no one had seen him for more than a year, and might still come out to assume power or resume his normal life as a businessman. I was deep in thought, walking away from the car, until I reached my mother's grave. The sight of her tomb reminded me of my last conversation with her less than two months ago. I had begged her to come to the United States. I had told her that her life was in danger for openly opposing the military government. I had reminded her that a government that could have been callous enough to publicly execute an international environmentalist like Ken Saro Wiwa was capable of unleashing unlimited terror on anyone or any group of people. But my warnings, which she described as the ranting of a child, fell on deaf ears. She ignored them just like my father had done and raised the tempo of her campaign for his release.

I began a short prayer for her during which one of my uncles, a stern-looking man wearing a black traditional Nigerian cap and a white kaftan, suddenly appeared. His cold response to my warm greetings jolted me. "What is the purpose of this trip?" His voice was harsh and his gaze furious.

"What is the purpose of that question and who gave you the right to ask?" My response was swift, my voice shaky.

He forced a smile, after a few seconds, probably out of fear that things would degenerate. "I am worried about you and your brother. Your mother's enemies are still around and if we take chances, they might just end up..."

"They might end up doing what? What can they do that they have not done already? Those foolish people who only know how to hit in the dark. I am not scared of them and I never will be." I was very emotional and my voice was loud because I was shouting.

He paused for a while before looking at me the way one would look at a mad man. Then he hugged me, something that I had expected him to do from the beginning. That was when I cried for the first time since my arrival. I became so emotional that I excused myself even after he had told me that he had come all the way from his house, a long distance, when he heard that I was coming. He urged me to spend some time with him. "We have so many things to talk about, I have a lot of information that would be of immense benefit and interest to you. Let's sit down and talk!"

I insisted on leaving and politely asked him to discuss with my brother before entering the house then my room. I was very tired indeed and was fast asleep within less than an hour. The time was only 6pm then but, to my surprise, I slept for a very long time, waking up at 4:30am the following morning. And, strangely, the first thing that came to my mind was my uncle's question: what was the purpose of this trip?

My first step was to secure my mother's assets which, in a lawless country like Nigeria, required my physical presence. A presidency can easily be stolen in Nigeria, talk less of material assets like land and pharmaceutical products. The Nigerian judiciary at that time, and maybe even now, was weak and far from being independent.

I sat on my bed, thinking about my mother, who had been one of Nigeria's biggest female traders in pharmaceutical products. Her dream was to become an industrialist and, for that purpose, she had acquired several acres of land on which she planned building a state-of-the-art pharmaceutical factory a year before my father's election. She was now gone, thanks to politics in a barbaric country, along with her dreams. But what baffled me the most early that morning was why my father had refused to declare himself as president from outside Nigeria. His tough experiences in life during his childhood should have made it clear to him that his gamble was suicidal.

He was born in poverty and tasted the harshness of life at an early age, trading in firewood when he was only nine years old. He carried the firewood on his head for hours, moving through long distances because he could not afford to hire a vehicle to transport it. That was why people joked, after he had grown up, that the firewood that he had carried on his head was the reason that he had no hair at the front of his forehead.

But despite these initial challenges in life, my father never gave up. He formed a musical band as a teenager, after his firewood business collapsed, to fund his high-school education and excelled academically, at the same time, which won him a scholarship to study accounting in the United Kingdom. From there he returned to Nigeria and rose in his career as an accountant, working at a hospital and the Pfizer corporation, until he reached the peak of his career following his appointment as the managing director of ITT Nigeria. He retired from ITT as the head of the American telecom giant's biggest branch in Africa, making a fortune before he was forty years old. That was how he was able to finance the costliest campaign in Nigerian history less than two decades later.

But my father knew that his gamble was a big risk, for he had once told me several years before his election that taking power from a dictator was like grabbing a sword from a crazy warrior. "You have to be careful or the sword can end up in your belly. Dictators are violent people whose trust you can win only by being excessively modest."

Fed up of thinking, after more than two hours, I performed my morning prayers then forced myself to sleep, wondering why such terrible things always happened in Africa.

Chapter Two

The following day

My mother had died exactly forty days ago and, in line with the Islamic tradition in Nigeria, my brother and I attended a special prayer for her. This prayer, known as the forty day prayer, is such a symbolic prayer that some people even consider it as significant as the funeral itself. The soul of the dead, according to them, can only be put to rest forty days after the demise of the deceased.

That event was the primary reason behind the timing of our return the previous day. It lasted two hours during which only Koranic verses relating to death were recited and discussed as a form of consolation to loved ones left behind. The Islamic scholar delivering the sermon went as far as saying that the worst part of the least beautiful house in heaven was more glamorous than the best part of the most beautiful palace on earth, assuring everyone present that my mother was in heaven because she had fought and died for the truth.

That morning I was relieved that not all my family members attended the event, for I did not want to see some of them because of their actions before my mother's demise. They had blamed her for supporting my father's aspiration to reclaim his presidential mandate, ignoring the fact that my father had independently made up his mind to pursue his mandate. These people opposed my mother's unwavering support for my father's decision, leading to a family feud to the delight of the military junta.

This crisis reached a climax when the military ruler General Abacha blocked access to my father completely at a time in which a decision regarding his legal representation in the treason suit filed by the government against him was needed. My mother had wanted a prominent lawyer named Mr. Ajayi to remain as my father's lawyer but my brother Kola, from my father's late senior wife, wanted another lawyer named Mr. Williams to take over my father's case. My mother insisted that only my father could change his lawyer and, since my father was in solitary confinement and unable to declare whom he preferred among both lawyers, the rift expanded and blew out of proportion. It was in the heat of this tension that my mother was assassinated, leading to the arrest of Kola and some of my uncles to tarnish my family's image. All the accused were eventually released when nothing was established against them.

After the forty day prayer I began executing my plans. I was already sick of being in Nigeria and wanted to leave as soon as possible. I estimated that one week would be enough to secure my mother's properties and sell off the remainder of her pharmaceutical stock but I was dead wrong. The assignment lasted almost a month but I was happy all the same because I would be back in the United States before the summer was over.

I booked a return ticket for August 15 and never for once contemplated trying to see my father. I did not think I stood a chance because my mother, and many other family members, had tried to see him and failed. Even though my trip had been short, it had been long enough for me to know that Nigeria was under siege. It was governed by an autocratic regime that was ready to suppress any revolt, a paranoid military government that was scared of its own shadow. People were afraid to come to my house, no wonder I rarely received visitors since my arrival.

Nevertheless I felt betrayed by these people and once called them hypocrites during a visit to an aunt. But she disagreed, "That is not fair.

How can you blame them? They love your father but why should they put themselves in harm's way? Even I am always scared whenever I go to your house and would probably not come if I was not your relative." My aunt went to her room and returned with a sealed envelope which she handed over to me. "You were not in the country when your father was arrested. That is why you know little about what transpired. Read the contents of this envelope and you would have a better idea about the intensity of the feud between your father and the Nigerian military government."

I became instantly curious, standing up to leave and wondering, at the same time, how an envelope so light could contain details so significant. I bade her farewell and went home at once, resisting the temptation of opening the envelope on my way. I entered my room and put on all the lights before looking at the content of the envelope. It was the full text of my father's presidential declaration speech entitled 'Enough is enough'.

I sat down to read it, word for word, and by the time I was done, I was terrified. I never knew that it was that long, that daring, that comprehensive. No wonder my mother had said that my father had told her that the speech would either lead to his presidency or his assassination. No wonder the military was so scared of a man who had never believed in violence, a man who had always worried about causing bloodshed. In that speech my father completely condemned all the years of military rule, an act for which I was certain that Nigeria's autocratic rulers would never forgive him.

Some key phrases of that speech jolted me. My father, for instance, described Nigeria's army generals to his audience as 'thieves of your mandate' whose 'remnants of patriotism' he had hoped to revive in vain through his efforts to 'climb the highest mountain, cross the deepest river and walk the longest mile' in order to get 'these men to obey the will of our people'.

But the most daring part of the speech came at the end when he castigated the entire period of military rule which had lasted twenty-four out of thirty four years following the country's independence. He accused the military of being responsible for all Nigeria's woes, citing the drug trade, civil war and credit card scams as major outcomes of military misrule and ended his speech with the slogan 'enough is enough' before a retired judge swore him in as the Nigerian president.

The only thing that I knew of that day, prior to reading this speech, was what my mother had told me on the phone. My father, 56 year old then, had climbed over the fence next to our soccer field and almost fell down in order to get to the venue where he made the speech. That was the only way he could have left our house on that day, July 11, 1994, because the military government had stationed over 600 police officers in front of our main entrance and exit. There had been strong rumors that my father was going to make that declaration and General Abacha was not taking any chances, my father had to be stopped at all costs.

But, despite the dictator's efforts, my father still made it to the other side of Lagos, a place named Epetedo, where he had chosen because of his love for the poor who inhabited that area, the real and down-to-earth people, as he always called them. They were the people on which he had spent the bulk of his wealth and for which he was now ready to die in order to defend the presidential mandate that they had given him. I was devastated after reading his speech several times and, by the following day, I had made up my mind to leave earlier than planned. There was no point staying there any longer. I rescheduled my trip and was set to go after three days until something happened.

An elderly strange-looking short man came to see me. He had big ears and a very small nose with bushy eyebrows. He wore old clothes and shoes but his tone was arrogant which made him sound like a rich man even though he was obviously poor. His eyes roamed around which revealed an inquisitive nature. "You are just as you were the last time I saw you. Nothing, I mean absolutely nothing, has changed." The old man was charming as well, I quickly noticed, after a conversation that had just begun.

I was sure that I had never seen him before but his name sounded familiar which put me slightly at ease. The only thing I found awkward was that he was too cheerful for someone on a condolence visit. I began suspecting that he had an ulterior motive and soon found out what it was. "Someone told me that you will soon be leaving Nigeria. I hope that is not true."

I nodded my head, confirming what he had heard, wondering who had disclosed my plans to him. "Knowing that I will not be able to see my dad, I have nothing else to do here. My further presence is a waste of time and, besides, I want to get back to New York as soon as possible and register for some summer courses."

He panicked and stood up. "You mean that you have given up so easily on seeing your father? Now that he needs to see you more than anything else. Only God knows what he is going through this very minute and here you are, talking about summer courses. What a disappointment you are!" His tone was condescendingly rude.

I felt guilty but stood my ground. "I am sure you know how hard my mother had tried to see him all to no avail. The whole world knows and yet you think I stand a chance."

He sat down once more as a cunning smile lit up his face. I am sure he knew that his words must have had an impact on me and that I was slowly beginning to explore the possibility of seeing my father. "You are more than you think you are, young man. But you don't know it, which is sad indeed." stated the old man sarcastically, adding. "Can you just imagine a newspaper with a headline stating that the government had prevented you and your brother, the sons of Kudirat Abiola, from seeing your father after her death?" He paused, his smile expanding. "The government cannot afford such negative publicity, especially now when it is trying to absolve itself from your mother's murder." His voice was convincing, his tone soothing.

With just a few words he had persuaded me and I was willing to give the prospect of trying to see my father a chance. But I still had some reservations. "Well, I guess it is worth a try. But so far, all what you have said is theoretical... The practical side of things will certainly be much more complicated." I was nervous. "For example, what should my first steps be? And through whom?"

I knew that not all people close to General Abacha could persuade him to allow me to see my father. A person capable of doing that must be someone whom he admired greatly or feared and the list of such people was tiny. I gradually started becoming pessimistic again as the wave of optimism generated by my charismatic guest began withering away. "You have things all twisted up, young man. It is the theoretical part that is complicated while the practical side is the easy part." He moved to a chair closer to mine, lowering his voice to almost a whisper. "There is a powerful man in the government who is from my village. Once he snaps his finger, things happen. You will see your father and no one would ever know how you were able to see him because the man, of whom I speak, is a discreet gentleman."

I became pensive indeed but doubtful as well because, if his words were true, where was this finger-snapping gentleman when my mother spent sleepless nights trying to see my father? Better still, where was this old man who is so eager to help me when she needed him? "In that case, should we get tickets and leave for Abuja this week?" I had made up my mind to go ahead with his plan despite my doubts and fears.

"No way! With all due respect, I will never enter a plane with you and your brother. What if the government decides to blow it up?" asked the man, shaking his head with a smirk on his face. But he quickly noticed my displeasure and added, "On a more serious note, what I meant to say was that going to Abuja by plane would be most unwise. We would spend a lot of money hiring cars. It is better for us to go with one of your cars and have access to a vehicle while we are there."

He was making sense although I was still pained by what he had said. "Okay then. If my brother agrees, we can go by road. I will talk to him now and get back to you shortly."

I rushed to my brother's room and told him everything. I knew he would concur because he was a much more optimistic person than me but I was not sure if he would like the idea of traveling by road. He was excited and did not mind embarking on such a long journey. I went back to the old man who smiled as he saw me approaching and asked, before I could utter a word, "When are we leaving?"

I had never met anyone as confident as this man but there was something else about him that made me feel uncomfortable, something that I had not yet identified. "Exactly three days from now will be perfect."

He stood up, a sign that he was about to leave, and we shook hands before he departed. That same day I visited a relative and informed him of our plans. He was worried and promised to follow us as a form of support which was a big relief because he was decades older than me and my brother. But a day before the trip he came to our house very early in the morning and cited family issues as the reason for not being able to accompany us. But he promised to keep us in his prayers and seemed glad, when he was leaving, because I had concealed my outrage over his decision. There was no point in making him feel guilty because I knew deep down that he had wanted to come. I escorted him to his car and watched him drive away until his vehicle was out of sight.

Chapter Three

Three days later

The day of my trip finally came. I woke up two hours before the departure time. I wanted to pray and visit my mother's driver Mr. Dauda who was still in a hospital following gunshot wounds that he had sustained on the day my mother was killed. He had heroically tried to move faster than her assassins but was unable to prevent them from catching up before they sprayed the entire vehicle with bullets.

I arrived at the hospital around 6am and waited on a chair in his room because he was still asleep. I began reminiscing about when this same man, who had worked for my family for almost fifteen years, used to take me to school. I was ten years old then. He always cracked jokes but he sometimes got on my nerves when he insisted on parking on the road to pray whenever it was time for prayers. I had always wondered why he did not just wait until we had returned home.

But one thing that saddened me that morning was that, despite his long years working for us, I had never visited his home. There was no justification for that because, aside from becoming a part of my family over the years, this man had risked his life to protect my mother. I felt anger mixed with guilt and promised myself that I would visit him at home before my return to the United States.

By the time it was 6:20am, just as I was about to leave for my trip, he opened his eyes. He was very weak but managed to smile. He sat up and wanted to talk but I did not want him to say much, for I had observed from a previous visit that talking had always put a heavy strain on him. But he insisted on having a conversation. "How are you, Abe?"

Abe has always been my nickname since I was very young. It was an abbreviation of Abiodun, my Yoruba name. I told him that I was fine and that I was on my way to Abuja to see my father. He looked alarmed which made me wish that I had not informed him of my plans. He performed a short prayer for me and had a valuable piece of advice. "The prayer of a traveler is always accepted so make sure you pray a lot during your trip."

I had never heard that before but I believed it and left after five more minutes. That was the last time I saw him because I was informed of his death before I ever saw him again.

My trip to Abuja began as a disaster. Abuja, being around twelve hours from Lagos by road, required that any serious traveler sets off early. That is essential, especially in view of the fact that there was always traffic, caused by big trucks and accidents, on the road. But even though we were supposed to leave at 7am we were forced to leave after a two-hour delay because the old man stood us up.

I was angry but my driver, who had always enjoyed the reputation of being the fastest in our house, assured me that he would still get us to Abuja on time before our 9pm appointment on that same day with the finger-snapping government top shot. The old man finally came at 8:55am and, just as we were about to leave, something else happened.

The old man had put his bags on top of mine in the boot of the car but I realized, just before we took off, that I had forgotten my books and walkman inside the house and dashed to fetch them. I returned in less than two minutes and kept a book and walkman on my seat in the car and opened the boot in order to put my other things in my bag. I pulled out the old man's bags in order to reach mine and that was when the wrap covering one of his bags slipped off, revealing a customized clock with the picture of General Abacha and a writing at the bottom that was full of praises for the despot. The old man's full name also featured somewhere at the bottom of the clock.

Treachery. I had experienced it a few times but not in such a brazen manner. I had never known that it could inflict such a sharp pain. I now knew how my father felt after being used by politicians as a bargaining chip to strike deals with corrupt military officials. That had been why a large number of his political party members had turned their backs on him within less than two weeks after his electoral victory was annulled. Most of these politicians had been bribed by the Nigerian military government, one after the other, and joined forces with the army to frustrate my father's dream of rebuilding Nigeria. One of them supposedly repurchased a castle that he had lost in the United Kingdom almost a decade before my father's elections. Others were helped by the government to pay off foreign debts. And even Kingibe, my father's elected vice-president, had bagged a foreign affairs ministerial position in the military government a couple of months before my father's arrest.

My mother had also been a victim of painful betrayals, for most of my father's so-called loyalists had abandoned her to continue with the political struggle all by herself with the exception of a few men like Wole Soyinka (a Nobel Prize Laureate), Segun Osoba, Ndubisi Kanu, Ayo Opadokun, Senator Tinubu, Dele Momodu, the Odumakins and a host of other activists. These people stood by her side in the fight against Nigeria's heinous despotic regime while others mocked her for rejecting financial settlement from General Abacha who had tried to buy her silence with huge monetary rewards and oil contracts.

My heartbeat accelerated as I removed my bag from the car and returned inside the house. I had lost interested in the trip but said nothing to the old man because confronting a man old enough to be my grandfather was somewhat of a taboo in Nigeria. But the old man followed me inside the house which left me with no choice but to be confrontational. The others, my brother and the driver, joined us as well as the man raised his voice, literally screaming at me, when he eventually caught up with me. "Go ahead and show your true colors. I knew that you were arrogant but not to this extent. You ought to be ashamed of yourself, young man."

I looked at him sternly, wondering from where shameless people like him got their pride. "Through the likes of you, evil dictators thrive since you are wolves in sheep clothing. It is you who ought to be ashamed of yourself."

He looked puzzled, everyone did. But, instead of saying anything else, I rushed back to the car and pulled out his gift to General Abacha and brought it inside the house. He glanced at it and quickly moved his eyes away before a smile full of guilt lit his face. He defended himself, declaring casually, "Oh, is this what this fuss is all about? All that talk about wolves in sheep clothing... Well I ..."

I interrupted him because, from the little I knew about him, he was capable of talking his way into or out of anything. "We had just agreed to travel three days ago and that is not enough time to produce this kind of gift. In other words, you have had it made for a while but were waiting for the right channel through which you could present it to your murderous general. What an inconsiderate man you are!"

I had wanted to slap him, for I had never felt so much fury against anyone standing at such close range. Another man might have buried his face in shame or withdrawn quietly but not this strange breed who maintained a straight face and spoke gently. "I will not be angry with you because I would be angry as well if I were in your shoes. In fact I think I deserve your anger because I was wrong to have kept something like this to myself despite my noble intentions." He sat down and breathed heavily as if he was worn out, probably in search of sympathy then, all of sudden, he quoted a popular Nigerian proverb."If you want to catch a monkey, you should behave like one." Then he went on to add, "That man, General Abacha, is a monster. All he cares about is money and prostitutes. But if I have to give him a clock to touch his heart so that you can see your father, so be it! What is a damn clock in comparison to the bigger picture, your .."

I interrupted him as my anger reached a new height. "I see. Then you have been deceiving us all along. It is Abacha, and no one else, whom you want us to see."

He could not deny my accusation. I flinched at the thought of meeting General Abacha face to face. I knew that merely seeing him would put my life at risk because, as an experienced soldier, he would sense my hatred and become threatened which might make him contemplate eliminating me. My fear reminded me of medieval kings and their fondness of executing their immediate rivals then wiping out their entire families.

At this point some of my domestic staff intervened and calmed me down. They sounded irrational as they stupidly claimed that the devil was trying to distract us from the noble goal of visiting my father. They added that the old man, even though he had a good purpose, erred by not disclosing his plans to me and my brother. And the old man, meanwhile, regained his voice and pleaded with me, promising to stick to the original plan and jettison the idea of seeing General Abacha. "Maybe this is how God wants it." started the man, warning, in his final bid to get me to rethink, that we would be taking a much longer route then shrugged his shoulders, "But what choice do I have since your wish is my command? Maybe this is how God wants it."

Nigerians are fond of using God as an excuse to justify bad things or crimes committed by them. A negligent doctor would say that he would not have made a careless mistake during an operation if God had not willed. Even the supporters of the military president who annulled my father's election were fond of saying that their mentor would not have been able to do what he had done if God had not approved his action.

I still wanted to call off the trip but decided to go ahead. But I had something important to do before we left. I picked up the clock from the table, took it to the kitchen and threw it into the trash can, generating a sharp noise when it broke into pieces. I watched and wished that the government of General Abacha would also break into pieces.

Chapter Four

That same day

After we left I become somewhat cynical about the journey, for I had literally coerced myself to embark on it. I was also angered by the fact that there was so much traffic and hardly any petrol on the way. By 10am, more than one hour after we had left my house, we had not gone beyond the outskirts of Lagos because our tank was empty and there was no petrol in sight. Buying petrol in filling stations in Nigeria's major cities at that time, despite the country's massive oil reserves, was as difficult as spotting a bat in broad daylight.

But we were lucky to stumble on someone selling petrol on the black market just before postponing our trip to the following day. Black market petrol is mostly of bad quality and thus capable of destroying a car's engine but we were willing to take the risk because we had no choice. The seller noticed our desperation and charged a ridiculously exorbitant price which we paid instantly without bargaining and filled our tank and jerry cans with petrol.

Scarcity of petrol was so common in Nigeria in those days that whenever Nigerians utter the word 'scarcity', they were referring to petrol even though the list of scarce essential items was endless then. We finally had enough petrol for the entire trip but, once that problem was solved, another one popped up. We were stuck in traffic caused by a major accident involving two trucks ahead of us. The traffic lasted almost two hours but, once we were out of it, the trip turned into a lovely experience.

For the first time in my life I saw the beauty of Nigeria's landscape at close range and this brightened my mood. Traveling such a long distance by road opened my eyes to a country that I had never known existed, I felt like a tourist in my own country. I remained wide awake throughout the journey, admiring almost everything on which I laid my eyes, starting from the similar-looking beautifully designed huts of different villages we passed through, huts painted in the same color, divided from one another by the same distance. Huts that had people in front of them, sitting on straw mats spread across the floor, drinking from cups, chatting and laughing apparently unperturbed by the burning sun.

Then there were modest-looking churches and mosques, most of which were either painted white or yellow, surrounded by people waiting patiently at their entrances and exits. I wish I had come with a camera, for I feared that I would not see the same sights again even if I traveled through the same road on another day. I also saw beautiful fields along the way, far away from the towns, most of which were empty but well maintained. I wondered why they were empty as we drove past.

Even the Fulani herdsmen, dreaded by many in Southern Nigeria, walked cheerfully with their cattle on that day. One of them waved at our car as if he recognized one of us. I was the only person who waved back because everyone else, apart from the driver, was fast asleep. But the most touching aspect of that trip was the sight of some little children in a place called Ogbomoso. Most of them were selling food, ranging from fruits to bread, while the others were idle, gazing and waving at us with their tiny hands until they were out of sight.

Once in a while we stopped to pray and stretch our legs and, in such occasions, were warmly received by local inhabitants who wanted us to spend the night in their town. But the old man, widely awake by then, always got angry and later explained that those places were dangerous because people lured naive visitors to stay in order to cut their heads or slit their throats at night for superstitious rituals. I did not believe him. I did not trust him but had forgiven him for what he had done earlier because, in such high spirits, it was the easiest thing to do.

We had been joking and laughing before we reached Abuja but once the driver announced our arrival, there was tension in the car. I looked at my watch, something that I had avoided doing as much as possible, and was angry that the time was already 9:30pm. We were late for our appointment. I notified the driver who doubled his speed and, after exactly twenty-five minutes, we were in front of a massive white house with black gates and plenty of trees. Some soldiers stood outside, scrutinizing our car suspiciously as the old man hurried towards them. He spoke to them for more than a minute and, because our car was far away, we could not hear their conversion until one of the soldiers shouted, "I have told you already that your name is not on our list. Your old age is the only reason that I have not yet slapped you." He raised his gun to frighten the old man then added. "Now get lost!"

My heart sunk. The old man returned to the car reluctantly. He was embarrassed but tried to feign being in control of the situation as he pulled out his phone from his pocket and dialed a number. But, just before his conversation began, he stepped out of the car. He did not want us to hear anything but I quietly sneaked behind him and eavesdropped out of curiosity. I discovered that he was not the link to the government official, as he had falsely claimed, but he was merely a link to another link. And since I could not hear the words of the person on the other line there might even have been a third link. I sneaked back to the car, my head spinning, and did not bother disclosing anything to the others.

After a while the soldiers forced the old man to end the call and instructed us to leave at gunpoint, an order that we enthusiastically carried out. "We should go to a hotel and get some rest." My brother was cheerfully trying to douse the suffocating tension in the vehicle.

"Things will go well. I am more convinced about that than ever before, for God is in absolute control, ruling from his throne." blabbered the old man before resorting to another Nigerian proverb, "Relief always comes after hardship has gone."

His phone rang. He answered and screamed after a few seconds. "Thank you! That is exactly what we will do." He hung up and tapped the driver on the shoulder, "Take us back to where we are coming from and drive as fast as you can!" He looked directly at me, adding, "Did I not tell you that God is in control? You are about to see the light of Zion."

I had no idea of what he meant by the light of Zion but nodded my head all the same. I was suddenly excited once again as the driver made a sharp turn toward the opposite direction and the car moved like a rocket. The road was not even a highway but no one bothered to caution the driver, everyone was too optimistic to think that anything bad would happen. My thoughts drifted toward my father who was detained somewhere in this town. I wondered where he was as I felt a sudden urge to comb every building in Abuja in search of him. My biggest fear, thinking of my father that night, was that he would give up the struggle for which my mother had sacrificed her life. Aside from spending a large portion of her own personal fortune, she had rallied the international community to support him.

In a meeting organized by Walter Carrington, the US ambassador in Nigeria, she had met with John Shattuck, the man responsible for human rights issues at the US States Department, and had briefed him about human rights atrocities committed by the Nigerian military government. She had also been on her way to the Canadian High Commission to pressurize the Canadian government to do more for my father's release when she was gunned down on June 4, 1996, on the seventh anniversary of the Chinese Tinanmen Square Massacre. I knew that my father had the right to make his own decisions but I worried about what my reaction would be if he were to abandon the cause. I did not want that to happen but, at the same time, I wanted him to come out alive and knew deep down that his release would likely be impossible unless he gave up his presidential mandate. I was confused and did not know what I really wanted him to do.

All those thoughts disappeared when I saw our destination from a distance. The same soldiers were stationed at the front of the house but, this time, they saluted us when we came closer and instructed their counterparts inside the house to open the gates. A secret service personnel directed us to turn right and drive all the way down to the very end. We followed his instructions and parked our car where he had specified. Another soldier appeared and escorted us to a pathway after which we were received by a maid who led us through a glass door into a massive sitting room full of pictures and medals. The old man pointed at a picture on the wall. "That is your savior. He is the man destined to help you see your father."

I was stunned, for I knew the man and was aware of his powerful influence. In a particular picture he stood next to General Abacha and the two of them posed like bosses in an Italian mafia. We all remained standing because, after such a long trip, no one wanted to sit down. All of a sudden there was a very loud voice from behind, "You don't have to be on your feet to look at those pictures." Our host was standing behind us, a short chubby man with big eyes and mighty lips. He was wearing gym clothes that were too small for him. "It actually makes more sense to sit down because you have a better view of everything in the living room from where the chairs are."

The old man introduced us to him, one after the other. He became very jittery after we all sat down and started saying some very strange things. "Here they are sir. I am glad to be the one to bring them. It was a lot of work convincing them to come." He stopped briefly, probably to catch his breath. "One of them even described you as a tiger because of your strong character, sharp mind and powerful will. But I told him not to worry because behind your firmness, there is nothing but kindness. I told him, you can ask him. I told him."

I was speechless. I had never heard such nonsense in my life. But our host seemed to have another opinion, he was pleased and probably believed all that nonsense. He smiled like someone listening to a sweet melody which encouraged the old man to carry on with his shameless flattery. "General Abacha is lucky to have the likes of you working directly with him. I know he has a vision but it is people like you who have the solution. That is why your success will always be real and never an illusion."

I felt very uncomfortable about the direction the encounter was heading and decided to intervene immediately. "Sir, I am pleased to meet you. It is kind of you to receive us. I am...."

But the old man interrupted me, he probably feared that I would steal the show or say something that might upset our host. He looked at me sharply before declaring to our host, referring to me. "He is a very traumatized young man so I will speak on his behalf."

Our host nodded approvingly and, from my interactions with some people serving in that government, I knew why. Their guilt always made them reluctant to deal with me directly and our host so far had proven that, for he avoided looking directly at me and my brother throughout our visit and shifted attention from himself by focusing on my father. "He should have walked away from politics because government was ready to compensate him." He paused as a big frown appeared on his face. "He is much more important than any president would ever be, he should have known that. He should never have sacrificed so much for a position beneath him." His gaze was fixed at the old man. "Even as a junior officer in the army I used to hear about how he appointed Nigerians to serve as ministers in other African countries. He even traveled to the United States without his passport and was allowed to enter that great country. Who else, apart from him, could have done something like that?"

I smiled when I remembered that incident. My father was allegedly quoted to have said on CNN that he was already halfway in his private jet when he realized that his passport was in his bedroom in Nigeria.

Our host continued ranting about my father. He sounded like an innocent observer, and not an active player in the government. And the more he spoke the more he distanced himself from the military junta. He even went as far as criticizing the way that my mother's murder was being investigated. "Even her case, look at how this government is handling it! It does not even know the proper way to..."

But the old man stopped him from completing his sentence, which infuriated me, and thanked him once again for receiving us before bringing up the purpose of our visit. "I know that through you, they can see their father. I even told them that once you snap your fingers, they will see him. How soon can that be possible, sir? We just arrived Abuja and await your signal."

The man looked surprised. That was when I realized that he was not aware of the purpose of our visit. He even had fury in his eyes and did not respond until after a while. I told myself, at that point, that he would not have allowed us to enter his house if he had known the purpose of our visit. "I can't be of much help in that regard. Many people in government have started pointing accusing fingers at me. They say I am supporting Moshood Abiola. They say I am an enemy to General Abacha." His voice was shaking as if there was an internal struggle taking place within him. "By the time I table your request to General Abacha he would finally conclude that I am a spy." He looked at me directly for the first time then quickly looked away. "Come to think of it, you don't even need me. There is a police officer in Abuja who is in charge of your father. He is a nice man and can be of help. This government is decentralized for efficiency so I would not be surprised if that man can bypass General Abacha and take you to your father."

He forced a smile then grabbed a pen from a table. He wrote the man's name and address on a piece of paper and handed it over to me. My brother and I thanked him and stood up because there was no point spending more time in his house. But the old man had not yet given up. He urged us to sit down, praising our host continuously, before pressurizing him to help us to see our father.

Our host was no longer amused by his praises. He frowned and rose to his feet. He entered a room and returned with an envelope full of money which he gave to the old man, adding,"This is for them, just in case they need anything while they are in Abuja."

I considered his gesture as an insult and my wrath increased as I watched the old man grab the envelope. Once again, my brother and I stood up and thanked our host for his advice, assuring him that we would visit the police officer the following day. He smiled but still avoided looking at us as we walked away. That was when I knew that seeing my father would require a miracle.

Chapter Five

The following day

I woke up before 5am the next morning but I did not have the slightest interest in leaving my bed. The disappointment of the previous night still weighed me down. My request was simple, my mother had died and I wanted to see my father, but even that was a big deal in the eyes of such a brutal regime. I am naturally a cynical person and was angry with myself for daring to be optimistic. I felt like a fool.

I performed my prayers and remained seated on my mat. I needed to think and concluded that strolling was the best way to do so. It was risky, though, because I did not know whether we had been trailed to Abuja but once the idea of a walk entered my head, I could not resist it. I had ample time for a very long walk because my brother and I had decided to see the officer by 10am that morning which was still a few hours away.

The sun was already out by the time I was on the streets. I began analyzing the political climate in Nigeria, as I moved along in the hot weather, based on all that I had learned since my return. I wanted to be as objective and realistic as possible in order to have a clearer picture of what my expectations should be regarding my father. And, after walking for more than half an hour, I arrived at a painful conclusion: ousting General Abacha from power at that period in Nigeria was virtually impossible which meant that my father was doomed because General Abacha regarded his incarceration as vital for his survival in power.

He was too paranoid to release him and his cronies, knowing how his mind worked, capitalized on his fears to ensure that he never considered setting my father free. One of them serving as a secretary to his government had allegedly warned him that their administration would crumble within five hours once my father was released. These greedy cronies had too much at stake, they were acquiring properties all over the country and abroad like their boss was doing, raising the level of corruption sharply to an unprecedented level. Not only was the state treasury being looted to buy assets, assets belonging to the state were being looted because they were given to top government officials in exchange for a fraction of their value.

The junta was not guided by ideology, all that mattered was making and squandering money, and jailing and assassinating opponents. And what made General Abacha a particularly dangerous man was that people underestimated him. He was calculating, and not daft as most people including my father had assumed, and derived his major strength from that misconception. I concluded that, after rising from the lowest ranks in the army to the very top, this evil dictator had the Nigerian army all figured out and had used it to put the country firmly under his control through the implementation of an effective set of strategies.

He starved the country of funds as a means of maintaining a grip on everyone, including his loyalists. He refused to release funds for months, even for projects captured in the budget, and resorted to all sorts of excuses such as audit, reviews, putting the country at a standstill in terms of federal projects but General Abacha did not give a damn as long as his own personal projects were being executed. He was fond of directing the minister of works to fix a particular road leading to villages of friends, for instance, whenever they complained and ordering the minister of power to procure transformers for certain areas because women he was dating lived in those areas. Those were some of his ideas of what governance ought to be. But he made one wise move that prevented his government from being a complete disaster. He set up a petroleum trust fund and ceded its administration to the most credible leader in Nigeria's history, an army general named Muhammad Buhari. General Buhari, as most Nigerians had expected, executed meaningful projects across the country in an upright and transparent manner.

With time General Abacha became more elusive until he disappeared from everyone's radar. Not even his ministers and state administrators had steady access to him. But this also worked in his favor because it made him more unpredictable and thus more capable of keeping his subordinates on their toes. There were always rumors of an imminent general sack which he was neither available to confirm or refute. But in 1996, though, the threat became real when he dismissed twenty-seven out of his thirty state administrators. No official reason was given for their sack.

A sudden general sack like that could have backfired, causing panic that would have led to a coup, but General Abacha and his closest allies had no reason to fear because, during that period, they had deployed only general officers completely loyal to the regime to head all of the four mechanized brigade headquarters in Nigeria. That single move eliminated any chance of a military coup being successful.

The general public comprising the masses and activists thus became the only potential internal threat to Abacha's rule. The death of my mother was a deadly blow to civil society because many activists fled the country or went underground. Abacha knew that his level of support among the masses was low but he also had a plan that helped him boost it. He promised to create more states which made him seem sensitive to the wishes of Nigerians, for creating states has always been a potent tool in the hands of corrupt Nigerian leaders through which they further distanced the people they exploited from each other and satisfied their tribalistic yearning. Abacha had no intention of being left out of this game.

He made a firm promise to create additional states and later fulfilled it in 1996, increasing the number of states in Nigeria from thirty to thirty-six, and gaining tremendous goodwill from his action.

The international community, however, remained the major thorn in the general's flesh. His civil rights records had turned Nigeria into a pariah state but he did not give up on the possibility of turning things around. And the political instability in some smaller African countries provided him with a golden opportunity to do so. Through them he demonstrated his eagerness to help the international community to right the wrongs in those affected countries by an active participation in peace-keeping missions for which he was applauded by a number of world leaders who gradually began to open their minds to the possibility of working with his government.

After analyzing these factors that morning I could not help but admire my mother for battling such an evil despot. I was sure that she had not analyzed things from the angles I had because doing so would have taken away her courage. She had put up a good fight and had almost succeeded in bringing down the government shortly after my father's arrest when she coordinated a strike with the support of the brave leader of Nigeria's union of petroleum and natural gas workers. A fearless man named Frank Kokori who mobilized a strike of eighty thousand workers that almost paralyzed the government until it was crushed, spelling doom for the opposition.

I headed back to the hotel when I was tired and reached there by 8:30am. I immediately took a quick shower before a light breakfast and by 9:15am we were on our way to the police officer's office. Even though there was no traffic a trip of less than fifteen minutes lasted forty-five minutes because we needed directions. I was very nervous on the way, and when we arrived, because, apart from the officer's full name, I knew nothing about him. I had no idea of what to expect.

We parked our vehicle outside the building and, just before we entered, the old man called me aside, "I would like for you to do the talking." He told me why before I could ask, "I saw you speaking Hausa in the hotel lobby and the officer, judging from his name, is from the Hausa tribe. He would be pleased if you communicate with him in his language because Hausa people love speaking Hausa."

On a normal day I would have willingly carried out his suggestion but on that day I was infuriated by it. My father had won the presidential elections because all tribes, including the Hausa tribe, voted for him. His victory was the primary reason that he was in jail and now, in order to see him, I was advised to please someone belonging to a tribe that voted for him by speaking to him in his language. The ethnic division that my father had defeated through his broad victory was now being used against him. Some powerful Northern elites had spread false rumors that he was going to divide the country and some people foolishly believed them, rolling back the gains of an election in which my father, a southerner, defeated his northern opponent in his opponent's own state and thus broke the jinx of ethnicity for the first time in Nigeria's history.

I nodded my head approvingly at the old man to avoid a new conflict, "As you wish. I will speak to him in Hausa with the accent of a native speaker." I declared obediently.

We inquired about the man's office and received directions from a young police officer. We walked fast and got there quickly, hoping that he had not gone out. We barely spent a few seconds with his secretary before being ushered into his office. We were surprised because we were not even asked about our identity. The secretary hinted at him, a dark-skinned fat man with a pointed nose. He was chatting with a guest and stood up at once when he saw us. He did not ask us who we were. That was when it crossed my mind that he probably knew that my brother and I were sons of Moshood Abiola.

I noticed a sad look on his face as he shook our hands. I sensed a genuine concern which I appreciated. We introduced ourselves and he quickly responded, "I know who you are."

After saying that he dismissed his guest with a wave of his hand then led us to a set of chairs. I was the first to speak, in English and not Hausa, and told him what we had come for. I also mentioned the name of the government official who had directed us to him while the old man looked at me, shaking his head, as if to say 'you will never learn'.

The officer's eyes lit up as if my words were a light switch. "Of course your wish will be granted. Such things are automatic and why shouldn't they be? Your mother has just died and, as a Muslim, you have the sacred right to see and condole your father. You can also console him." He paused as if he had just remembered something and quickly added, "It is also your right to be condoled and consoled by him." As he was talking, he noticed our excitement and smiled broadly, revealing a very yellow set of teeth. "I would have taken you to him right away but you know how these things are. There is protocol but don't worry! Today I will see General Abacha and get his approval and tomorrow you will see your father. You have my word."

That was exactly what we had wanted to hear. We all stood up and began shaking his hand, one after the other. The meeting was like a fairy tale. We thanked him, bade him farewell and were on our way out. He had not told us the time to come the following day but I knew that I would be there by 8am and did not mind waiting until midnight to see my father.

Once we were out of the building I wanted to scream out of joy. I suddenly realized the importance of having a father more than ever before and began regretting times in the past when I got upset because he had ordered me to run errands simply because I had wanted to go out with my friends. That day I wished I could go back in time and be a better son.

That same evening I went to a Lebanese restaurant to celebrate. I was alone because my brother did not feel like going out. I was so excited and ate food that was enough for three people. Even the owner of the restaurant gave me a warning look when I placed the order. I ignored him and ate without thinking. But as I left the restaurant, after eating too much and barely able to carry myself, I realized that what I had just done was one of the dumbest things that I had done in a very long time.

Chapter Six

That same night

I took a short nap when I got to the hotel that evening and found it difficult to sleep throughout the rest of the night. Maybe I was too excited or maybe I was too restless. My brother and I might be the first people to see my father in almost two years, I reminded myself, knowing that the poor man would feel guilty about my mother's death. I began thinking about ways of making him realize that her death was not his fault. He had wanted to keep her out of his political battle at first but had gradually allowed her to play a major role when the burden of the struggle became too heavy for him to bear on his own.

I had never encouraged her active involvement in the struggle because it was too risky and dangerous a gamble for a woman with seven children, none of which was an adult by then. Another reason why I discouraged her participation was that my mother, because of her pure and kind heart, had always been incapable of detecting treachery and evil, and these are two things present in politics than in any other field.

Not being able to lie down or remain seated without being restless prompted me to roam around my hotel room. I had plenty energy to burn and even wanted to go out jogging but I was scared to do so because of the darkness outside. My brother, on the other hand, was more relaxed when I went to his room. He was praying and looked like he was meditating. He had always been more religious than me and I admired him for that. I prayed with him but stopped every now and then because I was convinced that our prayers had already been answered.

I left his room and went downstairs to the hotel bar, not to drink, but to meet people and listen to good music. I was happy for taking that decision because I had a wonderful time with some very interesting foreigners with whom I discussed about many things until 2am that morning. The following day I did not eat in the morning because of my heavy meal the previous night. I took a quick shower and was all set to go to see the officer. I went to pressurize the others, one by one, for us to leave earlier than planned but the old man laughed. "Do you think you are in America? Over here, no one occupying that kind of position comes to work before 10am because such people work until late at night."

Deep down I knew that he was right but I still wanted to leave early. "What if we go and wait for him? We have nothing to lose.. Or better still, my brother and I can go now and you can join us whenever you are ready."

"No way! We came together and we will do everything together. Don't forget that all this progress was my handiwork. After all, I was the one who introduced you to the man who gave you the idea to see this officer. You have now grown wings and think you can dump me."

At first I was speechless because I thought he was serious then I burst out laughing when I realized that he was joking from his facial expression. I left him and went to the hotel restaurant and forced myself to eat because I was so restless. I bumped into one of the people whom I had encountered the previous night and we had a fruitful conversation about the irrigation project that had brought him to Nigeria. I left him after half an hour and headed back to my room but on my way back, I saw the others at the lobby. I followed them to the car immediately because they were all set for us to go.

Someone had parked in front of our car, however, and had made it impossible for us to move out. We waited for almost an hour before the owner of the vehicle showed up and we were finally able to exit the hotel. We reached the police station quickly and entered the building. I was almost tempted to run inside because I was so impatient but, just as the old man had predicted, the officer's secretary informed us that he had not yet come. He led us to a waiting room where we spent almost three hours that felt like three days.

In my boredom my mind drifted back to the previous day when the old man had advised me to communicate with the officer in Hausa. I shook my head because his advice was a sign that the military government's propaganda about my father being a sectional leader had been effective and I knew why. This was easy because, since a bloody civil war in the 1960s, Nigeria has been an ethnically divided country for decades.

My father rolled out his campaign and ignored the fact that Nigerians were also divided along religious lines by doing something that was described then as political suicide. He yielded to pressure from some influential governors in his party and picked a Muslim as his vice-presidential candidate despite the fact that he, my father, was a Muslim as well. Ideally the Christians, who form around half of Nigeria's population, would have ensured his defeat but they believed so much in his message and voted for him, putting religious considerations aside. This was a major shock to Nigeria's military leader at that time who had believed that my father would lose the election.

It was in the middle of these thoughts that the officer finally came to the waiting room. Once I laid my eyes on him, I knew that something was wrong. His gaze was burdened with melancholy and his body seemed lifeless as he sluggishly shook my hand. He told us that he would see us after five minutes but did not send for us until after more than an hour.

By the time we were ushered into his office, he did not ask us to sit down. He stood up and remained standing in a clumsy manner as if he was about to fall down. I could tell that he wanted our stay to be as brief as possible. After we had greeted each other, he finally confirmed my fears. "Timing. Those entitled to make a decision on your matter don't have the time to do so at this time. State matters have overwhelmed them. It is the therefore the timing that is the problem and not them. If you had come last week or even the week before, things would have been different, that much I know."

He sounded like a recorded rehearsal. His voice was cold but his look was gentle and full of remorse. Where was the cheerful man who had filled me with so much optimism less than twenty-four hours ago? He had now turned into a pale man who reminded me of defeat and the tragedy that had engulfed my life. Was my father still alive? If he was then why was it so difficult for anyone to see him? Probably feeling uncomfortable about the lingering silence in the room, the officer swiftly added with a slightly more energetic voice." But on my own part, I can still do something."

For a split second I thought that all was not lost. Maybe he had made up his mind to smuggle us to where my father was. I watched him closely and tried reading his mind before he spoke. That was how impatient and desperate I was. "I can take a letter from you to him. Yes I can. Then I can also bring a letter from him to you. That is almost like seeing him, isn't it?" He tried to look jovial but failed. "At least there would be a form of communication, which in essence, is the purpose of your visit to Abuja."

Letters. I looked at him deeply. Did he just say letters? Controlling my rising anger was indeed an epic battle. I wanted to tell him that he is a hypocrite pretending to have a conscience. I wanted to tell him that people like him were the tools through which evil men like General Abacha carried out their diabolic machinations. I wanted to tell him that if all officers in positions of authority like him had stood by the truth, General

Abacha and his corrupt team would have been history long ago. At that point I hated him as much as I hated Abacha because I believed that he had been insincere when he previously displayed concern, he had been merely acting a script in a devilish plot.

But I said nothing because giving him a piece of my mind would have been meaningless. He was a puppet, a useless puppet. "Okay, we will write him letters. Can you give us some paper and a pen?"

I believe that my mind must have been working on its own whenever I think of that day. I was too dazed to think as he opened his desk and pulled out some paper for my brother and me. He was so elated as if he truly believed that writing letters would have mended our broken hearts. I took the paper from him without looking at him or thanking him. Then I went to one corner of his office to draft a long letter to my father. My brother did the same after going to another corner. Then we handed the letters over to our host who smiled and promised to deliver them to our father.

We bade him farewell and, just as we were about to step out of his office, he started muttering something. "Make sure that you come to-morrow because there might be a letter from him for you. I am sure there will be because he will certainly write... And maybe soon you would all meet and never part again. With prayers anything and everything is possible."

His voice sounded distant even though he was not far away. It was like an irritating noise coming from the middle of nowhere. The previous day I had a lot of respect for this officer. I had considered him a saint among devils which made him seem larger than life but today this same man had become smaller than an ant. I was too disappointed to say anything, too disappointed to ask him when I should come the following day because I did not care anymore.

Chapter Seven

The same day

That was it. It was over. I had finally given up. There was no way I would ever see my father again unless through a miracle, which was impossible. I was being too cynical which was the last thing that I wanted to be but did I have a choice? If being cynical was the only way that I would have peace of mind then being cynical was not such a bad idea.

Once again I blamed myself for believing that I would see my father and for not calling off the trip after I had stumbled on the clock. It was a big mistake, I repeated to myself, then I became confused. Would I not have been angry with myself if I had not come? I was tired of thinking. I decided to do something productive, something that would push those pessimistic thoughts out of my head before they drive me mad. That was when I opted to visit a childhood friend whose father was a civil servant in the federal government. They had moved to Abuja a couple of years ago when the city became Nigeria's capital.

My friend and his parents were ecstatic to see me. His father was a very tall fair-skinned man with slanty eyes and his mother the exact opposite, a smallish woman with a dark complexion and a large forehead. The entire family received me warmly in their very humble house in the outskirts of Abuja. They invited me to have lunch with them. I accepted their invitation and, aside from good food, I had a lovely time. His father brought up a lot of fascinating topics, ranging from ancient Yoruba history to African literature which made him seem more like a philosopher than a civil servant.

I admired them because they were obviously a very happy family. I felt strange about that because, when we were younger, my friend was the one who admired my family. He used to tell me that I was one of the luckiest people on earth. That was how we developed a very strong bond but now the tables had turned and I was the one who envied him despite the fact that he lived in such a tiny and plain house. My priorities had changed, for I now realized that contentment and peace of mind, and not money and power, were the authentic benchmarks of success.

My mind started working like a clock two hours later after I had re-turned to the hotel. That was the opposite of what I had hoped for when I decided to go out. That day I concluded that if I were given a choice in life to determine the circumstances of my birth, I would rather be the son of a carpenter or any other laborer as long as I would not undergo what I was currently experiencing. I wanted to trade away being the son of the rich and powerful man whom many people believed installed presi-dents across Africa, a man whom many people believed gave out huge monetary donations representing just a tip in the iceberg of his immense wealth, a man whom many believed had the habit of depositing a million dollars into the account of each child fathered by him at birth and a man whom some falsely claimed was the head of the CIA in Africa, despite his denials, a CIA chief whose permission was needed for the agency to act or react in the African continent. That day for the first time in my life I wished that I was the son of a poor or middle-class man.

We did not go to see the officer until late the following afternoon. His gloomy look was still there but his voice sounded more jovial than the last time we saw him. He had news for us. "I saw your father yesterday and told him that both of you are here. I gave him your letters but he refused to accept them. I even pleaded with him but he did not yield and insisted that I bring both of you to give him the letters by yourselves."

After that he handed the letters back to us. I was surprised about my father's action, surprised that he still believed that he was dealing with people with a conscience, people whom he felt that his approach would have forced to bring us to him. I wondered how he was able to cope with the news of my mother's death. I was sure that he had heard because his guards would have told him.

The last time that I saw him, shortly after his arrest, was in a police station. He had been brought there to see me, my brother and my sister, and after telling us to make sure that we study hard, he had declared that he would rather die than abandon his presidency. On our way out of the police station, two officers saddened by his statement followed us then scolded us for not convincing him to give up his struggle. Such sympathetic officers would have told him about my mother's death.

I wanted to tear the returned letters but managed to squeeze them into my pocket, thanked the officer for his efforts as we began our exit from his office. I was not as depressed as the previous day because I had already prepared my mind for the worst. But the officer reached the door before me and pulled out a tiny piece of paper, which he handed over to me, from his upper pocket. "I almost forgot to give this to you. It is the number of one of General Abacha's closest aides. He is always with the General." He paused then continued. "I told him what your father had said and he thinks that he can be helpful to you in the future. He would consult with the General from time to time and, at the appropriate time, the General would give the green light and the both of you will see your father. The General will grant your wish because he is a kind man."

He smiled broadly after he had finished but what drew my attention the most was the way he uttered the word 'General'. He made it sound as if he was talking about a war hero. It was pronounced in the same way that a patriotic French man in the 1950s would have pronounced the name of General De Gaulle. This same officer, just yesterday, was ashamed of his 'General' but today he sounded like he worships him. I felt disgusted and put the paper in my pocket before giving him a piece of my mind. "Tell the General that only God gives anybody, including him, the green light to do and undo things." I looked straight into his eyes and added. "The same way that only God gives us a conscience to help us do the right thing and follow the right people."

He did not respond but looked at the ground. I knew that he had gotten the message and left his office immediately. I never returned there again. The old man looked so worried on our way back to the hotel, this trip had not been worth his while at all, for he was neither able to see my father nor present his clock to General Abacha. But he still had one more trick up his sleeves. He called me aside once we had reached the hotel, "The problem between your father and Abacha seems unsolvable but a friend suggested something yesterday, something that might work." My gaze was indifferent but he proceeded. "My friend is close to a man who knows Abacha's children. The man has agreed to take you guys to them because he believes that once you guys become friends with them, they can help you soften their father's..."

I stood up and walked away. He was stunned and did not bother bringing up the matter again. The following day we left Abuja but did not return to Lagos until after a couple of days because we stopped by in another state. By the time we got to Lagos, I was glad to be physically far away from General Abacha. Before going home, we took the old man to his house where he gave me a very odd parting gift. He stared at my brother, with a gentle look on his face, and stated, "You are humble and

45

kind-hearted," then he suddenly set his gaze at me, with eyes full of scorn, and said, "As for you, all I can say is that you are a bloody motherfucker."

I was dumbfounded, for old people in Nigeria are hardly ever crude. I did not react until I was on my way home when I burst out laughing. That trip, from the beginning to the end, was an experience that I will never forget for the rest of my life.

Being back in Lagos made me look forward to returning to the United States. I made up my mind never to come to Nigeria again unless my father was released. But on a boring day, almost a month after my return from Abuja, I opened my travel bag, pulled out the number that the officer had given me and dialed it. A man answered and after I had told him who I was, he responded sternly, "A foreign leader is about to arrive in Nigeria as I am talking to you and he has insisted that General Abacha receives him personally at the airport. Such things happen all the time. That is why it is impossible for me to bring up matters such as yours to the General's attention until a much later date."

He went on to give me a lecture on the state engagements that the General had to cope with. Then he promised to call me when he has processed my request after which he hung up. I was not disappointed at all because I had stopped expecting anything positive from my trip. But I was surprised that he and the inspector pronounced the word 'general' with the same tone and excitement. It was obvious that the 'General' had brainwashed quite a number of people.

I threw away the number and made arrangements to leave for the United States right away, I did not want to spend more than one more week in Nigeria. But I left even earlier than planned after receiving a strange phone call from someone who refused to tell me his name, all he said was, "You will know who we are when we get to you."

That was how my trip ended. I learned a lot from that journey, perhaps more than from any other experience in my entire life. But the most painful lesson that I learned was that criminal leaders in third world countries can get away with crimes committed in broad daylight. General Abacha had claimed that he was not the one who annulled my father's elections and should therefore not be held responsible for it. But what if the General's only car was stolen from him by someone and given to another person, will the General allow the beneficiary of his car to enjoy driving it while he moves around on his feet, even if the beneficiary was not the one who stole his car?

Chapter Eight

"Why are you leaving through a Nigerian airport? You had better return to the United States through a neighboring country." warned my aunt after I had informed her of my plans to travel from the Muritala Mohammed Airport in Lagos. She sensed that I was not convinced and added. "You will never make it. The immigration officers will seize your passport. They will humiliate you and, maybe by the time they are done, you would be compelled to complete your education in a Nigerian university."

Out of all the things she said her last sentence caught my attention the most, for I had only one semester left before graduating. She sounded so confident like someone seeing my future in a crystal ball. "But what difference will it make if I leave the country through a neighboring country?" I asked nervously. "The immigration officers stationed at the borders are even tougher than those at the airport because they are meant to curb smuggling. They are worse than their counterparts at the airport."

She gave up and changed the subject to a completely irrelevant topic, a sign that she was furious. My uncle's wife also came on a visit and, from the moment she entered my living room, I knew that she was annoyed and soon discovered the reason. "I find it hard to believe that your trip to Abuja was so fruitless, I find it hard to believe that it was a complete waste of time. I find it hard to believe that all that risk was for nothing."

I, on the other hand, found it hard to believe that she was blaming me for not being able to see my father. I was devastated. "Yes it was all a waste of time and that should not be so hard to believe because, as you very well know, Nigeria is being governed by a very ruthless man. But maybe if your husband had come along, and not backed out a day before the trip, we might have been able to rub minds together and miraculously devise a way to make the trip fruitful. I hope you find that easy to believe."

"Do you remember that we told you not to come to Nigeria?" snapped my uncle's wife. "You young people think you know everything but you know nothing. And now, instead of being apologetic for not accepting sound advice, you are grandstanding." So that was what all this talk was about, a fallout from the fact that my brother and I insisted on coming to Nigeria against the wish of most of our relatives. Her comments so far, though painful, were bearable but the next thing she said made me lose control. "History always repeats itself. The same way we warned you not to come to Nigeria was the same way we warned your mother not to follow her husband blindly. How can a woman make such a huge sacrifice for a man who has three other official wives and a host of concubines?"

I knew that my mother had done a very rare thing for a man who, as the woman accurately stated had many women in his life, but I also knew that winding back the clock of time was impossible and, as a result, her comments were malicious indeed. "My mother was unique and you have just proven that in view of your insinuation that most women would not have done the same for a polygamous husband. My father, on the other hand, was not a perfect husband, he was a womanizer. He had even made a fortune through his connections in the army but all his faults can never wish away the fact that he is the legitimate president of this country and that he is smart and generous enough to change this country for the better." I paused then proceeded. "So because my father was not a perfect husband, should my mother have remained quiet while those criminals detained him, moving him from one deplorable cell to another? Should she have been quiet when they drove him around at night in tinted vehicles in order to break him down psychologically? Should she have been quiet when they paralyzed his businesses, causing thousands of people to lose their jobs?"

Both women began begging me to stop as I continued to pose more questions, causing a very dramatic scene. I refused to stop shouting until they gave up and left. I was remorseful then and really wished that I had not over-reacted. Once I calmed down I sat down to analyze my aunt's warning and wondered whether I would be prevented from traveling at the airport. The thought was scary but taking that risk was still more appealing than contemplating a long trip by road to a neighboring country, especially in view of the fact that I would be traveling alone because my brother was not in a hurry to leave Nigeria.

My fears reminded me of how my father had been prevented from leaving the country several times before the election. His passport had even been seized more than twice which was part of the negative signals that were coming from the then military president, signals that should have made it clear to him that the general did not like him and was only deceiving him when he urged him to contest in the election. The General's legendary skills in twisting people around was, among other reasons, what earned him the nickname 'Maradona' because of the soccer player's dribbling prowess.

These thoughts still on my mind, I decided to focus on my final urgent task in Nigeria. My siblings and I had decided to seek political asylum in the United States and I needed to gather facts that would prove our eligibility. Finding relevant newspaper articles to support our bid was easy because my mother kept a bunch of them in her room, articles with which she had used as exhibits to substantiate her allegations against the government to the international community.

It was during my search for the most striking of such articles that I learned for the first time that my mother had been detained for one night shortly before her death. The military junta had accused her of funding the distribution of anti-government pamphlets around Lagos, inciting people to revolt against the government. There was a picture of her on the newspaper, sitting on a chair with an alarmed look on her face. I was too distraught to finish reading the article and simply threw it, and all other articles I found, into my suitcase without bothering to select the best ones.

The day of my trip came faster than I had expected. I would never have thought that traveling out of Nigeria could be so frightening as I approached the airport that afternoon. The same airport from which I once traveled with my father for a weekend in London. That trip had angered my mother because I was not yet on vacation. "That should not be a problem," insisted my father, adding, "All he needs to do is to bring his books along and study on the plane. We will be back in Nigeria on Sunday so that he gets to school early on Monday."

Things went according to plan but my mother was still upset after we had returned because she felt that my father was spoiling me. Today, though, I felt more like a fugitive and certainly not a prince, at the airport. I was given my boarding pass quickly and I was thrilled that I was allowed to check in my suitcase without being asked to open it. Some secret service officers standing by the ticket counter would have raised an alarm if they had seen the large quantity of political articles in my suitcase.

There were some other secret service officers cracking jokes by the entry section designated for only intending passengers. They ignored me as I walked past them. I was pleased and never knew that being ignored could ever feel so nice but my joy was short-lived. "Why are you walking so fast? Come here and show me your passport." ordered a loud voice from behind, causing me to freeze for a few seconds.

I looked back and was surprised that the man who had instilled so much fear in me was tiny indeed, he had a long beard and very mean-looking eyes. From his accent and appearance I knew that he was a Northern Nigerian Muslim and instantly remembered the old man's advice that speaking Hausa to northerners always had a positive impact on them. I decided to give it a shot with this man whom I strongly suspected was a secret service operative. "Asalam aleykum wa rahamatulahi wa barakatuhu!" I purposely greeted him the Islamic way, making my greeting longer than usual as a form of distraction and a display of confidence. He was startled, he probably did not think I was a Muslim because of my short-sleeved shirt and pair of jeans. "I was walking fast because I did not want to miss my flight. Here is my travel document." I spoke in Hausa, using the word 'travel document' instead of 'passport' intentionally to impress him with the depth of my knowledge of his language.

He took the passport and was waving it, staring at me. "Where are you from and how come you are speaking Hausa?" But he added apologetically before I could reply. "I did not even reply your Islamic greetings, I am sorry about that. Wa aleykum salam wa rahamatu lahi wa barakatuhu!"

"I am from Ogun State. I learned Hausa through a language course in the United States." I was smiling as I replied in Hausa even though his questions were in English.

I had told a big lie. My mother had grown up in northern Nigeria and had taught me Hausa when I was eleven years old. The man began grinning and nodding his head continuously. He finally brought my passport closer to his eyes and was about to open it, the last thing that I wanted him to do. "Is there a mosque around here?" He shifted his gaze from the passport towards me slowly then nodded his head before I added. "I hope it is not too far from the terminals because I would like to observe my afternoon prayer there before my trip."

He returned my passport immediately. My strategy had worked. He grabbed my hand delicately as if I was a blind man crossing a road and hurriedly led me to a spot from where I could see people praying in a group. "It is not a real mosque per se but it is the closest we have to one. Hopefully we would have a more befitting venue by the time you return on another visit."

I thanked him and said goodbye then walked toward the prayer section. My flight was still hours away and I strongly hoped that I would not bump into him again or any other security personnel. I boarded the flight easily after a few hours and, at that point, I regretted refusing to use the Hausa language to communicate with the police officer in Abuja. Doing that might have made a difference by persuading him to go the extra mile to help me see my father. That was the last thing that crossed my mind before my flight took off.

Chapter Nine

After a month

New York. I had never felt so much love for a place in my entire life. I had chosen to go to New York University because it was in Manhattan, the capital of New York. Manhattan provided the ethnically diverse environment that was lacking in Connecticut where I had gone to high school. It was very lonely being in Kent, my school in Connecticut, because only a few Africans studied there. I felt disconnected from my country and continent. But I was lucky to have friends in New York back then and realized, through my visits to them, that New York was where I wanted to study after high school.

I only stayed on campus during my first two semesters at NYU. I got my own apartment within a year after my arrival in a place called the village situated in downtown Manhattan. I always invited people to my apartment in those days. I needed company to distract me from the sadness that overshadowed my life, sadness that clung to me like a parasite because of terrible memories that had become part of my negative reality.

News from Nigeria always made me depressed but, strangely, I always looked forward to hearing them. In this regard I was like an addict unable to resist the lure of a destructive drug. I held onto the hope that sense would find its way out of all that madness as I waited anxiously for any information coming out of Nigeria. That was when I learned, for instance, that a judge had stepped down from my father's case because he did not want to tarnish his reputation. That could only mean that the conspiracy against my father was becoming thicker. Those fears were confirmed when his trial became permanently stalled as the military ruler began his long anticipated march toward democracy. In a bid for legitimacy General Abacha allowed the registration of five political parties as proof of his willingness to promote democracy which, to me, was evidence of his readiness to replace his army uniform with civilian attire.

After a while I became more miserable and needed more than having company. I needed to be engaged in an organization, or a company, where my mind would be occupied. I wanted to acquire the necessary skills and experience to succeed in the United States. I had no plans of returning to Nigeria unless my father was released and, from the look of things, that was likely never going to happen.

To this end I got in touch with a family friend who made contact with a personal friend and that was how, a few days later, I was on my way to see an African capital investment topshot, an impressive man who had built a solid career in a major American investment bank. The man was to offer me an unpaid internship and I finally had something positive to which I could look forward. An internship in the United Nations would have been more ideal for me because of my flair for languages but I was told that only candidates with a Master's degree were eligible for an internship in that organization.

I was not nervous on the day of the interview because I had been informed that it was already a done deal and that the meeting was just meant to be a formality. I was somewhat surprised, though, because I had thought that such things only happened in countries like Nigeria where having connections was mostly the key to success and not competence like in the United States where one must be somewhat qualified to even work for free.

I was very excited when I arrived the man's office, for I believed that every step forward was an additional step toward the American dream and farther away from the Nigerian nightmare. I spoke to his secretary, a dangerously attractive woman, who confirmed that she was aware of my appointment but added that he was in a short meeting. She led me to a glamorous and spacious waiting room that resembled a conference hall in an ancient European castle. She noticed that I was smiling as I admired my surroundings and told me that all their clients are mostly impressed by that particular waiting room. I wanted to say that I was more impressed by her than the waiting room but changed my mind when I noticed a gigantic ring on her finger.

I was there for at least thirty minutes after she had left. The place, just like other parts of the building that I had seen, was furnished with antique furniture. The color yellow played a dominant role in the waiting room and was the main source of the sharp, glaring brightness. Being there inspired me. It made me think of success. It made me covet it. All successful people I had met narrated a different version of how they had succeeded. I knew because I have always asked questions about journeys to success. I wanted to know because I wanted to be successful. But my father's story, out of all the different stories that I had heard so far, was the most fascinating and my conclusion had nothing to do with the fact that he was my father.

Success is mostly connected to timing, and not just hard work. My father took advantage of a time when the Nigerian military government was interested in doing business with multinationals that had indigenous Nigerians at their head. He was able to recover debts that the government owed ITT, the company where he served as the Nigerian controller, and once he did that, he was able to convince the company's management to make him the managing director of its Nigerian subsidiary and allocate almost half of the company's shares in Nigeria to him.

My host entered the waiting room quietly as I was deep in thought. I did not hear the door open or sense his presence until he spoke. "Anyone there? Come on, snap out of it!"

I was shocked to see him. I was very embarrassed and stood up to greet him. I knew that he was the man whom I had come to see even though I had never met him before. He was of medium height and had a brown complexion. He wore a very thick pair of glasses that made him look so intelligent and made me wonder if he had a library stuck inside his brain. "Good morning sir! I am so sorry, I must have been daydreaming." I stated as I shook his hand. "It is certainly not my fault that this enchanting waiting room has mesmerized me." We both laughed. I was still very embarrassed and, as usual, hid behind a question. "I am fascinated by the color yellow but your company seems to be too fascinated by it. Is there a mystery behind that?"

"Our interest in that color goes way beyond fascination, it is more of an obsession, and, trust me, there is no mystery behind that." declared my host, sounding smooth like the skilled salesman that he probably is. 'Yellow is a bright color, it makes people optimistic which makes it easier for us to sell our services to them. Only optimistic people invest from the bottom of their hearts." added my host, smiling as he asked me to escort him to his office.

We walked fast and quickly got there. "I was told that you want an internship." I nodded my head, surprised that he had gone straight to the point immediately after we were seated. "Why do you want to be an intern when you can have my job? I am just a step away from being a vice-president."

I was rattled by his question. "You are a senior executive in a major financial institution and I am a university student who does not even have a degree yet. Are you mocking me?"

He burst out laughing then he suddenly looked serious. "Yes I am a senior executive and you are still a student, I agree, but let me explain something to you." declared the charismatic investment banker, moving his head closer to mine. "Your father is one of the richest men in Africa. He is your ticket to my job. All you have to do, young man, is to find a way of getting some of his wealth from wherever it is to this institution and I guarantee you on this beautiful day in the city of Manhattan that you would have the same rank with me in this company before you blink more than once."

Chapter Ten

I am sure that the look on my face was blank. I had come on an internship hunt but now it was I, the hunter, who was being hunted. His attitude reminded me of the cunning old man back in Nigeria and my respect for him vanished. He was no longer a role-model who had achieved the American dream but an opportunist whom I wished that I had never met. I was certain that he was hinting me indirectly, by bringing up this particular matter now, that the unpaid internship, and not only the job offer, depended on my ability to access part of my father's wealth which he would invest through his company.

I did not know how to begin explaining to this aggressively ambitious man that, even if I strongly believed in his idea, having access to my father was impossible, talk less of giving him documents that would authorize such an investment. The Nigerian government might even think that he was about to fund a coup.

After a while I responded, making a strong effort to be as polite as possible. "What you have said sounds very interesting. It is an excellent idea because I am certain that anyone investing in this company would never have a reason to regret." I paused to arrange my thoughts. "But my father is in solitary confinement. He is incommunicado because the government is determined to keep him isolated from the entire world. No one has seen him in so long and, frankly speaking, no one knows if he is alive." My host looked distraught indeed. He was obviously disappointed at my response and a lingering silence ensued which made me feel very uncomfortable. I decided to give him a reason to be hopeful even though I knew that his request was hopeless. "But he has a lawyer in Europe, a lawyer who has some powers to act on his behalf. The lawyer might not be able to effect a gigantic investment as you would wish but he is in a position to do something that is somewhat reasonable."

He smiled broadly as if I had just saved his career which made me wonder if there was ever a limit to targets given to financial consultants in such companies. A man in his position, after climbing so high up the corporate ladder, should have had enough clients by now to keep away desperation so why was he so desperate? Why was he so inconsiderate to the extent of exploiting someone like me whom he knew had just lost his mother and whose father had been locked up by a criminal regime? I was not an expert in his field but, if I were in his shoes, I would have offered the internship first then, after a few weeks, brought up this other issue casually as if it was a coincidence. I never wanted to see him again.

"I am sorry about what happened to your mother, may her soul rest in peace. I know that the long arms of the law will catch up with the culprits and they will be punished." He had finally said something reasonable. "We have had our own share of political tragedies in my original country as well, maybe such political tragedies are the only thing that African countries have in common." I agreed with him but he changed the topic before I could respond. "Should I call the lawyer directly? I think that would be a great idea because I have all the information that he would need on my fingertips. It can even be a conference call of which you can be a part, marking the beginning of your training in our organization."

I was taken further aback by his crude aggressiveness. I had once read that financial consultants in firms like his were given a target of ten million dollars every two years but from the way this man looked and sounded I would have believed that the target was much more than that. I politely told him that I will talk to the lawyer myself first because of his conservative nature then return within a week for us to call him together. He seemed pleased with my response but I was not pleased to be in his office. He, on the other hand, looked very relaxed and obviously wanted a longer conversation as he continued assuring me of a bright future in his firm, repeating the same things over and over again. He even suggested that we go into business together, trading in African commodities and building hotels in South America, promising to give me more details the next time we meet.

At that point I stood up and wanted to leave but he objected. "Not now, please stay a little longer." I reluctantly agreed then he added. "Let's talk about Nigeria! I know everything about your country. Do you know that?" He laughed and spoke again before I could respond. "I mean it. I literally know everything about Nigeria." Then he dropped a bombshell. "Reparations for blacks because of slavery. Sponsoring that initiative was the biggest mistake that your father has made in his entire life." There was a deep silence then he continued. "Your father turned from a friend of the West to a foe once he got involved in seeking reparations and an African politician's days are numbered once he ceases to be an ally of the West."

I was startled. I had no actual details of my father's involvement in that initiative aside from the fact that he had spent a fortune on it. But, looking back, I don't think that it was a worthy initiative for two major reasons: it was unfair to demand financial settlement from the West for slavery because the actual culprits had died long ago. Furthermore, such a settlement, if given to blacks as a whole as my father was advocating, would have generated a sharp conflict because the American and Caribbean descendants of slaves have a right to lay claim to all of it. My father, however, did not see things from that angle and even tried to secure the participation of black American congressmen in the initiative.

"Don't you think you are exaggerating when you assert that reparations turned my father to an enemy of the West?" The mere thought of that was frightening. "After all, from my understanding of the whole thing, that initiative was more of a plea and certainly not a demand." I tried to sound normal to cover the panic that was building up inside.

"The West will never allow a man with such a revolutionary idea to assume the helms of affairs in Nigeria, Africa's most populous country and, of course, the custodian of the world's sixth largest oil reserves." He had a very stern look on his face and was about to say more but was interrupted by someone who informed him that his attention was urgently needed. "I will be right back. Don't move an inch." He hurried out of the door as I began analyzing all that he had said.

Chapter Eleven

I was very eager for my host to return. I had not heard enough even though I knew that his remarks would probably cause me more pain and tension. General Abacha, according to him, was not my father's only enemy as if that was not bad enough. The West had also turned against him and would never want him to rule. That meant that my father was fighting a completely hopeless battle, I painfully concluded, because I regarded the West as my father's last hope.

No, that can't be true. My host was wrong because, if he was right, then why was the American Ambassador in Nigeria so receptive to my mother when she fought for my father's cause? After all, as a diplomat, he could have insisted on dealing only with the government that was actually in control of Nigeria. He could have ignored the opposition as many other diplomats had done. Furthermore, if the West held such a grudge against my father, then why did so many Western ambassadors attend my mother's funeral at such short notice? Almost all of them were present at her burial even though they had been notified just a few hours before the event. The event was like a state burial.

There were other signs confirming that my host was wrong. General Abacha has always complained that the United States had become hostile to Nigeria since 1993, the year that my father's election was held and annulled, which means that the West was angered by what had happened.

My host re-appeared, breathing heavily, as if he had come back in a hurry. "Now where were we?" He settled down on his chair, adding. "Your father should never have disclosed plans like reparations until he became the president. He let the cat out of the bag too damn soon."

Once again I disagreed. "He was just being honest about his opinion and, by the way, he was not really thinking about becoming the president when he began sponsoring that initiative. It is wrong of anyone to connect that initiative to his later presidential ambition because both matters have never been tied together."

"A settlement for slavery will never see the light of day, whether as a result of a plea or demand, and that is the plain truth." declared my host in a resolute tone. "I am a realist and I like calling a spade a spade."

"I agree with you wholeheartedly." I was being sincere. "Finding a sharing formula among the victims of slavery would have been harder than getting the West to agree to a settlement. But the initiative can be used to urge the West to consider debt relief."

My host was pensive for a while. "Your last point is reasonable indeed but you still don't have a firm grasp of what is at play. Haiti had a similar problem as Nigeria, its elected president was ousted, and we all know what was done by the West to restore the man to power. Why has the same assistance not been extended to your father? After all he is also an elected president. This brings me back to my initial point: the quest for reparations was a destructive decision."

This time he was completely wrong. The president of Haiti was a sitting president while my father remained an elected president after falling victim to a sinister plot. I gave him a better idea of that plot by narrating how an organization called 'The Association for a Better Nigeria' had been sponsored by the military government to gather signatures to prevent my father's election from taking place. I described how the organization was able to secure a court ruling to stop the elections two days before it was scheduled to hold and how, when the electoral commission decided to go ahead with the election, the same organization was able to secure another court ruling to stop the electoral commission from announcing the results even though the election had already taken place. "By that time, the commission had already released the results in almost half of the states in Nigeria and my father was in a clear lead, he had so much of a lead that he would have still won the election even if his opponent secured all the remaining unreleased results." I paused for a few seconds. "But my father was not officially declared the winner because the electoral commission was barred from declaring the complete results. This, and not reparations, is why the West has not been able to help him."

"Maybe you have a point. You have a much better understanding of this topic because it is about your country and your family." An expressionless look appeared on his face. I was certain that he disagreed with my analysis but just wanted to end the discussion amicably.

We spoke about a few other less sensitive issues and I was relieved when his secretary announced that he had another visitor. I stood up immediately, he rose as well and shook my hand. "It was a great pleasure meeting you. I look forward to managing some of your father's assets and working with you."

"The pleasure is all mine." I replied cheerfully before reminding him of my visit the following week, a visit I knew would never happen. He smiled broadly and looked at his calendar before picking a date that was convenient for the both of us. I knew that I would never see him again and I never did.

When I woke up the following morning I called a man who had known my mother since her childhood and had worked closely with her and my father for a few years before her death. I knew that he was one person capable of providing answers and I needed answers. I was still agitated from my conversation with the investment banker. I dialed the man's number, forgetting about the time difference between Nigeria and the United States. "Are you alright? First of all, do you know what time it is here?" From his tone I could tell that he was angry.

I looked at my watch and realized that the time difference between Lagos and New York had skipped my mind. I was calling him at 3am Nigerian time. "I am so sorry. I would call back in the morning."

He objected before I could hang up. "No, never mind! I am fully awake now." I could hear him moving, perhaps he had been lying down and was now sitting up. I felt guilty and was about to apologize again but he continued talking. "You did not answer my question. Are you alright?"

"I am not alright. I was with someone yesterday and he told me something that really terrified me."

I narrated what the investment banker had said about reparations, putting more emphasis on what he had told me about my father and the West. He waited patiently for me to finish talking then he said that he would call me back from his wife's mobile phone, a more secured line.

Five minutes later my phone rang and it was him. "The point raised by that man is something that your father himself was concerned about. The reparations program was never meant to be solely his initiative, it was meant to be an initiative sponsored by him in collaboration with the Nigerian government. But your father discovered, after he had begun funding the program, that the government was not interested at all. That was how he ended up financing it by himself and, frankly speaking, he did not have much of a choice because, since his name was already associated with it, his reputation would have been destroyed if he had done otherwise."

"Does the West consider him an enemy? Will it work against his release because of that initiative?" I was worried about the answer.

"I don't think that the West will work against his release but they would likely not be very enthusiastic about his attempt to retrieve his stolen presidency. That initiative was too controversial. Many people advised him to distance himself from it but he did not listen. He was being wrongly advised to get more involved in it by a Caribbean diplomat serving in Nigeria and some other people." He sighed then added. "Focus on your studies and excel, these matters are too big for a twenty year old."

We both laughed then I thanked him for his detailed response. He promised to call me if he had any more information and hung up. I was motionless for a while then decided to stop thinking about the matter. There was no point because my father had done what he had done and there was no going back.

Chapter Twelve

A few months later

After the death of my mother the domestic part of the Nigerian democratic struggle suffered a major setback. My father had initiated the struggle but it was my mother who had sustained it. Once she was gone, the loss of morale in the ranks of human rights activists in Nigeria can be likened to the loss of hope in the ranks of warriors in ancient battles after the sudden death of their leader in combat. The anniversary of the elections, whose results she had sacrificed her life to uphold, came only eight days after she had been killed, a few weeks before my trip to Nigeria. But that year, the anniversary was very dull, for she was no longer around to draw attention toward it. I was happy that I had not yet arrived in Nigeria to witness the neglect of that day. The international aspect of my mother's democratic struggle, however, witnessed a major boost, thanks to my sister Hafsat who had turned into an activist. She had my mother's courage and was the most vocal among her seven children.

I, on the other hand, was gradually becoming more of an introvert. But I used to socialize more whenever I traveled outside New York. During a trip to Washington D.C. I was introduced to a Nigerian who, after realizing who I was, had good news for me. "Congratulations! The opposition radio in Nigeria has been named after your father's late wife. It is now called Radio Kudirat."

I was thrilled and thanked him for that piece of information without informing him that Kudirat Abiola was my mother. I was tired of people condoling me and wanted to move on with my life. I later learned that the men behind the radio station, under the leadership of a very principled man named Kayode Fayemi, meant real business. The station aired the atrocities of the military regime, exposing its human rights violations and massive corruption to an international audience, just like my mother had been doing when she was alive. Without the station such revelations would never have been known because the military government had arrested so many journalists and thus greatly weakened the media's ability to serve as an effective watchdog. Even journalists' wives were not spared whenever the police could not lay hands on their husbands. They were detained and treated like common criminals. Some of them were raped.

I was proud indeed that Radio Kudirat was the most authentic source of information about the catastrophic developments in Nigeria at that time and that, since its exact location was not known, the military could not eliminate it as it had eliminated my mother. Radio Kudirat was thus immortal. I was basking in euphoria, unaware of another positive development that was about to unfold.

One day I met a Nigerian friend waiting for me in front of my building. I was returning from a pharmacy with some drugs because I was not feeling well. I needed to get some rest and showed my friend the drugs, pleading with him to return another day or choose a day for me to pay him a visit. He shrugged his shoulders, "I have wonderful news for you but I guess that the good news can wait until another day."

He turned around and walked away but I caught up with him, grabbing his hand and dragging him inside the building. "You had better have some very good news because I am not strong enough to be dragging you like this."

We went up the elevator. No word was spoken but I knew that he had excellent news from the look in his eyes. We got to my apartment and settled down on the sofa. "The city of New York has decided to name the corner of 44th street on second avenue after your mother."

"Oh my God!" I shouted that expression over and over again. I could not believe my ears. At long last my mother was getting international recognition for her bold opposition to an evil regime. "But why is the city of New York so interested in her? She never lived here and was hardly ever known in this part of the world." That was my way of verifying the authenticity of his information, my investigative and cynical mind was on high alert.

"The city of New York has done something similar in the past. It named the street on which the South African embassy is located after Nelson Mandela during the Apartheid struggle."

It was a major source of pride to me that my mother was being compared to a great man like Nelson Mandela whom my father knew very well and from whose rise to the presidency of his country my father had received the courage to fight for his own presidential mandate.

I remember the day in which my father, after his return from Mandela's inauguration where he said he had received a presidential treatment, told some people that, "If Mandela could be brave enough to risk spending 27 years in prison then why should I be scared of going to jail? Why should I be scared of water if I was bold enough to go near the river? Is the Nigerian military government as powerful as the former Apartheid government of South Africa?"

My mother too had been inspired by Mandela's former wife, Winnie Mandela. A day before her death, my uncle had visited her to inform her that someone in government had warned him that her life was in imminent danger. Her initial response had been that even if she were to be killed, it is not a big deal because not all warriors go to war and return alive. But she later apologized to my uncle for her outburst and told him that she would be less critical of the government. And to further put his mind at rest, she told him one more thing. "Governments, no matter how brutal they are, never kill women. Winnie Mandela, for instance, fought the Apartheid government of South Africa for decades and was not killed."

But I was initially disappointed with the approach of the South African government in confronting General Abacha's human rights violations. It adopted a policy of subtle diplomacy. It sent renowned personalities like Desmond Tutu to plead with the military to release my father but I had wanted a more aggressive approach from President Mandela. But I later realized that the reason why Mandela had played such a subtle role was that there was no way he could have put more pressure on the Nigerian government. South Africa had no major direct dealings with Nigeria through which Mandela could have exerted pressure on Abacha. By the time his diplomacy had failed to yield the desired results, my confidence in him was restored when I read his description of the Nigerian military regime. "We are dealing with an illegitimate, barbaric, arrogant military dictatorship which has murdered activists, using a kangaroo court and using false evidence."

News of the street naming continued to be a source of immeasurable joy to me. I planned going to that street at least once a week to look at my mother's name even though my apartment was not close to 44th street. But one day a friend called me with some very bad news. "Can you imagine what is happening? The Nigerian government has sponsored a group to go to court in order to stop the city of New York from naming the street after your mother."

I paused, trying to remain as calm as possible. I asked him if he knew the grounds on which the group was establishing its case. "Their argument is pointless. They are claiming that naming the street after your mother would embarrass the Nigerian government." He paused briefly. "But the only good thing that has come out of this nonsense is that the government has exposed itself. It has made it clear to the whole world that it should be held responsible for your mother's death."

Chapter Thirteen

After the suit was filed the judge halted the naming temporarily and fixed a hearing on the case. The Nigerian government shamelessly swung into action, launching a battle of many fronts through a delegation comprising of its ambassador to the United Nations and some other senior officials of the Nigerian embassy, in order to stop the naming of the street after my mother.

There were very strong rumors that the military government spent a fortune on these efforts, doling out huge sums of money to rented crowds paid to demonstrate against the naming, crowds that included many people who were not even Nigerians. I once joined the crowd, out of curiosity, to see and hear things by myself. "Comrades, it is time for us to call it a day." shouted a bulky man with a Jamaican accent before adding, "Let's depart to our various homes in order to shine our amour and return tomorrow to ensure that this street is not named after that woman."

I was sure that he was not Nigerian and did not even know my mother's name. I saw him again, shortly afterwards with four other young men, walking behind a man wearing a suit. They all squeezed into a car and drove off. More unconfirmed details of the protests filtered in after a few days, revealing that each demonstrator received fifty dollars, news that shocked an American friend of mine who put things in an interesting way. "A dictator steals billions of dollars out of which he donates fifty dollars to a few of his victims in exchange for their moral support, what an excellent deal!"

In a related development a former American mayor David Dinkins and a nobel prize laureate Wole Soyinka attended the hearings and defended the naming of the street after my mother.

I wanted to attend the hearings as well but stayed away because the matter was too sensitive.

But, as the hearing progressed, I was worried that the Nigerian government would succeed in truncating the initiative because of the money it was spending. It had even paid a huge sum of money to an American to help thwart the street naming. The American even offered to fund a trip by members of the city council to Nigeria to hear the government's side of the story. But I received a major moral boost when I heard of the testimony of an American whom my mother valued dearly, an American whom she once described as the most principled diplomat that she had ever met in her entire life.

Walter Carrington, who had just completed his four year tenure as the American Ambassador to Nigeria, decided to lend his voice to the debate in his capacity as an individual and not as a representative of the United States government. He argued in favor of the street being named after my mother whom he described in the hearing as 'the bravest, most uncompromising woman Africa's human rights struggle has ever known.' He summarized her actions by stating that she 'took up the leadership of the struggle, not only to free her husband from jail but to free all Nigerians from the jackboot of military rule. Kudirat was the opposition leader the Abacha regime feared the most.'

The former ambassador painted a clear picture of the brutality of the Nigerian military government by giving a vivid account of how security agents, acting on the orders of the military regime, violently disrupted a farewell event organized in his honor by 'the human rights group whom Kudirat Abiola championed'. This action, he added, was in violation of all known diplomatic practices, lending a credible voice that further dispelled the false claims by the Nigerian government that activists were the ones responsible for the violence in Nigeria.

The court, after reviewing all the facts presented by both parties, ruled in favor of the city of New York naming the street after my mother to the dismay of senior diplomats of the Nigerian consulate who had worked fervently to prevent that from happening. That was how the corner of 44th street in Manhattan was named after Kudirat Abiola, a woman who had coincidentally died at the age of 44.

The Nigerian government, on the other hand, wanted to retaliate. It decided to name the street of the United States Embassy in Lagos after someone it assumed was a foe to the American government and, from a list of people including Timothy McVeigh and Mohammar Khadafi, it selected Louis Farrakhan. But that gesture was very short-lived because a democratically elected government later reversed it and renamed the street after Ambassador Walter Carrington.

I took two close friends to a restaurant near the corner to celebrate the occasion and we had a lovely meal before walking around the corner repeatedly. That day I told them a short story about how my mother had inherited her courage from her father.

During the May Riots of the 1960s Northern Nigerian protesters took to the streets of some parts of Northern Nigeria to demand the reversal of a government policy unifying the civil service and wrongfully killed a number of Eastern Nigerians living in the North. My mother's father, a Southern Nigerian who had lived in Northern Nigeria for many years, was not pleased about this development and decided to hide a popular Eastern Nigerian tailor in his house in order to sneak him to the train station where the man would board a train to his part of the country. My grandfather was able to hide the man for a long time because being a prominent goldsmith stopped his house from being inspected.

Once he felt that the coast was clear he decided to take the man to the train station, disguising him as a woman, but my mother insisted on following them because she had been the one cooking for the man since his arrival. Her father agreed reluctantly and they set forth together.

On the way my mother and her father walked slightly ahead of the man and were surprised to see so many road blocks set up by different mobs. They passed all of them successfully but the man become too scared and began walking slowly until he froze completely at the last road block before the train station. The mob became suspicious and removed his veil before beating him to death. My mother and her father were watching the horrific scene by then because they had looked back from a far distance and, on their way back home, they saw the corpse of the man who had stayed with them for almost a fortnight.

I also took my family on a trip to New York more than a decade after the historical street naming and purposely stayed in a hotel within walking distance from my mother's corner. I pretended, during a stroll with my wife and children one morning, that I was confused as we approached the corner. "I left my glasses at the hotel. Can anyone tell me the name and number of this street?" I had stopped and was pointing at the sign on which my mother's name was boldly written.

My son was faster than my wife and his younger sister Kudirat, named after my mother, and screamed the name of the street. This caught the others unaware and they stared at the sign for a few seconds in shock. That moment was the highlight of that trip and one of the happiest moments of my life.

After that we quietly returned to the hotel where my daughter asked a very important question. "Was that corner named after me or my grandmother?"

Chapter Fourteen

After a few months

The positive effects of the street naming lasted for a very long time. I became a much more optimistic person, ready to take on the world. Gone were the days in which I looked for excuses to indulge in lengthy study programs, claiming to be preparing for the future, when all I was doing was building a fortress around myself in my tiny world. I bought all kinds of language learning books from the Barnes and Nobles store opposite my apartment and taught myself several languages. I saw languages as something to be gulped with limitless passion and they soon became my sanctuary from a painful reality. But that was all over, for I had been extracted from that negative state of mind and set free from the bondage of melancholy.

I wanted to start my own business and was uncertain about the area that suited me until my brother came up with the idea of supplying customized phone cards to companies, phone cards that would carry companies' logos distributed as gifts to customers. These phone cards, aside from being attractively inexpensive for companies ordering them from us, enable such companies to thank customers for their patronage through a voice message before their calls are connected. I fell in love with the idea and my brother and I formed a company, named after my mother, called Kuditel Promotions. We were not the first company to offer that service in the United States but, based on our findings, that service was more popular in Europe then than in the United States.

Setting up a business, though, is more than having ideas and capital at the right time, it requires having connections. And that was something that we did not have in the United States. But that changed when an aide to my father reminded us of a man in Boston who had become my father's intimate friend after working closely with him at ITT during the 1970s. This man had stayed in the ITT group and was now the president of Sheraton corporation, a former subsidiary of ITT. I was given the man's number and would have called him right away but had to first sort out some domestic issues. I was about to move from New York to Virginia in order to stay with my brother and nearer to my sisters living in Maryland. They had been taking care of my mother's two youngest children and I also wanted to be of help in that regard.

I finally got in touch with the man after I had settled down in Virginia but was told by his secretary that he had traveled. She was very pleased that I had called, stating that her boss always spoke about my father. She gave me the company's address before I hung up and suggested that I send a detailed proposal to her boss. I did as she had advised the following day and waited endlessly for a reply.

One day, after several months, I received a phone call from Sheraton Corporation. The caller was a staff who wanted more information about our services and was calling from Boston but I told him that I preferred to pay him a visit. I was eager to take full advantage of the opportunity of the call and informed him that I could be with him anytime within the next five days. He sounded shocked and slightly reluctant but went ahead to confirm an appointment and gave me his address. I was taken aback by the fact that his office was not at the company's headquarters and wondered whether seeing him would be worth my while.

I rushed downstairs, trying to remain optimistic, and told my brother what had just happened. We rubbed minds together to devise a marketing strategy that would win us Sheraton's patronage. We drew up a list of the reasons that could make the company reject our proposal and another list of the reasons why the company would likely accept our proposal. Our hope was that the second list would be much longer than the first one while we tackle the issues raised in the first list.

These were strategies that we had learned from our father, a strategic realist, far from the excessive idealist some people later said he was. That night we went out for diner, a sort of celebration, but I was nervous indeed, in part, because the Sheraton staff had not mentioned that the president had told him to call and also because he had requested for more information even though our proposal had been extensively detailed. "The whole thing is a big mystery and that is not good at all. Business is like war, you have to know everything before the battle begins." I was suddenly emotional and confused.

"War? What are you talking about? We are going to sign a contract and you are talking about war." declared my brother, being optimistic as usual, even after I had told him why I felt uncomfortable. "Who cares whether the man shares the same office with the president or not? The important thing is that he called. That is all that matters. Thinking too much will give you hypertension someday."

After that we spoke about other things and waited for the day of our trip, a day that I will never forget for the rest of my life. I had never believed in luck, for I had always seen it as an excuse for lazy and incompetent people to justify their shortcomings. But I learned that I had been wrong on that day. My brother and I had already put our things in the car and were all set for our eight-hour journey to Boston but just before we left, I remembered that I had not switched off the lights in my room. I went back inside and heard the phone ringing upstairs. I climbed up and answered. "Is this Kuditel Promotions?" asked a man who later introduced himself as a vice-president in Sheraton. I responded, introducing myself as a director of the company. "Can you tell me more about the proposal that you sent to the president?" His tone was calm.

I was speechless for a few seconds, trying to gather my thoughts. "Yes I can, certainly, But, if you don't mind, I would rather do that face to face. I am on my way to visit my sister at Harvard today and would be glad to see you at your earliest convenience." I was anxious, trying to sound confident.

He paused for a few seconds then fixed an appointment for me to see him at 2pm the following day. I thanked him and hurried back toward the car to share the wonderful news with my brother but the phone rang again. I did not want to respond but changed my mind. It might be the vice-president again, I told myself, as I rushed back upstairs and grabbed the receiver. "Hello!" I was almost out of breath.

My high-school guardian was on the line, a Nigerian based in New Haven called Salisu Abdulahi. "Do you remember when you were hospitalized for malaria here in Connecticut after a trip to Nigeria?" asked my former guardian after greeting me. I told him I did and he continued. "I was sent a refund from the hospital, a check written in your name because you were apparently overcharged by almost ten thousand dollars."

"But I did not pay for it, my father did. So why did the hospital send the check in my name?" I was dumbfounded.

"Do you want me to send the check back to them? The address of the hospital is on the ..."

"No way, not at all." I almost got angry with him for making that suggestion. "Please send me the check. I have to go now because I am on my way to Boston by road."

"Why don't you stop by then? Connecticut is right in the middle of Virginia and Boston. Come and take the check yourself, unless you are coming by bus."

Once again, I found it hard to believe my ears. "In that case I will be seeing you in the next five hours. Just hold on tightly to that check." We both laughed and he gave me his new address then hung up.

We were in New Haven after a couple of hours and found him waiting for us in his living room. Locating his house had not been easy but I was happy to have come, not only because of the check, but also because I could see the progress that he had made in his life. I saw his new beautiful house, in comparison to where he lived when he was my guardian, as proof that the American dream was real and that it was within the reach of anyone willing to work hard and remain focused.

He invited us to a meal and gave me the check as we sat down. "Seeing is believing." I was staring at the check, "Even if what I am seeing is unbelievable." I concluded, putting the check in my pocket.

Chapter Fifteen

A few hours later

After eight hours we had reached Boston, we had taken a short nap and a shower in the apartment of a friend. Our first meeting with my first caller was less than two hours away and I was gradually becoming more nervous and worried. When I was younger I had noticed that my father was fond of asking nervous people meeting with him to return after they had calmed down. He had always feared that they would have said the opposite of what they wanted to say in their anxious state of mind. And that was the last thing that I wanted to happen to me during any of my meetings with the Sheraton officials.

I began a conversation with our Francophone hostess, hoping to relax. I asked her a question that had always been on my mind. "Why do most French-speaking Africans prefer living in Boston?"

"Why do you want to know?" asked my tall and pretty dark-skinned hostess, apparently surprised by my curiosity.

"If the answer is a big secret then maybe you should keep it to yourself." I replied jokingly.

"You are hilarious." declared the woman before adding. "I came to Boston because of its cold weather during the fall and the winter. I think that many other Francophone Africans came here for the same reason."

I repeated my question in French and she gave me the same answer. "I translated my question to French because I suspected that you did not understand my English but I was wrong. How can you come here because of the weather when this weather should be every African's nightmare?"

"I disagree. Cold weather is a good thing. It boosts the immune system and makes you smarter. I am sure you know that most inventors grew up in cold places." argued my hostess before adding. "What do you have against the cold?"

"The weather has nothing to do with intelligence or the immune system. I wonder where you heard that from." I paused then continued. "I began disliking the cold when I lived in Connecticut. The cold was so bad during the winter that I resorted to walking backwards to protect my face from the freezing wind. Now can you picture a scenario of a teenager walking backwards and worrying about the possibility of falling into a bottomless pit?"

She laughed for a very long time. "I can't picture that scenario at all and, frankly speaking, I don't believe that you ever walked backwards."

After an hour we were on our way to our first appointment. I was not nervous anymore, the conversation had helped. We arrived at our destination an hour early and were soon told where to find the man we were looking for. We reached his office after a minute and saw him seated on his desk. The office was tiny indeed, barely big enough for its contents, consisting of two chairs and a mountain of files. The man, blond and of moderate height, stood up at once when we appeared. "Welcome gentlemen! I am glad you made it. How was your flight from Virginia?" asked the man, putting on his suit jacket that had been hanging on his chair. He was agitated.

I spoke first after telling him my name. "It was not a flight, we actually drove all the way here and it was a great experience."

"And a long one too." added the man, shaking both our hands.

There was something warm about him that should have made me feel at ease but I was troubled. I was extremely bothered by the fact that his office, from what I had seen, alluded to his irrelevance in that corporation. Maybe the president, before sending our proposal to the vice-president, had not been interested and his secretary had asked this man to contact us on her own as proof that something was done.

The man brought in another chair from the next office and we all sat down before I spoke again. "You are right, it was a long journey. But it was worth it because we have met you." He smiled at my comment and we began our discussion.

My brother explained our product to him while the man stared at him as if he was hearing about it for the first time. Then my brother presented details that were on the proposal we had sent word for word as I studied the expression on the man's face to know if he was interested. He seemed enthusiastic. After my brother had finished I gave the man a newer version of our proposal and he opened it, nodding his head repeatedly. "This is an amazing idea. Our customers can see our logo, hear our message and be touched by our generosity at a cost of only one dollar and fifty cents. How awesome!" announced the man, grinning with his eyes still on the proposal. "I will follow this up with a report to our marketing department and a decision will be taken from there. All I needed were a few details which are in this new proposal, details that you could have given me without coming. I hope you have another important reason for being in Boston."

I was glad that I did have another important reason for being in Boston. I told him I did without giving him details then asked him a series of questions to gain something from our visit. By the time we finished that one-hour meeting I had an idea of the decision-making process in the company, the number of its hotels abroad and the general rules governing its domestic and global operations. This additional information, coupled with my company's agreement with a reliable service provider capable of offering competitive rates for Sheraton hotels in the United States and abroad, made me confident that I would strike a deal as we walked out of his office.

Chapter Sixteen

Three hours later

The drive to the Sheraton Headquarters was smooth, I did not even feel a bump on the traffic-free road. So far so good, I told my brother, wondering whether the day would end as beautifully as it had started. I began planning ahead, focusing on my next potential customers. The Marriot came to mind because, as a result of its bigger hotel network, it would offer more business than even Sheraton.

"How do you know if Marriot is bigger than Sheraton?" asked my brother after I had shared my thoughts with him. "There will even be a clause in the agreement between Sheraton and our company, a sort of exclusivity clause that would bar us from dealing with other hotels." He declared sternly.

"Do you know how many other hotels there are in the United States alone? That will not be fair at all, it will hinder our progress. I was pained as I spoke. "Maybe there is way around that clause, if it exists, because being subjected to something like that would be tragic."

"The only thing that is tragic now is listening to you put the cart before the horse. Here we are on our way to a customer and here you are talking about reaching out to that customer's rivals, instead of focusing on how to first secure a deal with the customer. That is tragic."

"Maybe you have a point." I declared after a while. He was right, for I was building castles in the air when I should have been concentrating on how to strike a deal that afternoon.

I remained quiet but my mind drifted to the future once again. The market for my product was huge. Even a small grocery shop can use customized phone cards to reward its loyal customers. I decided to market the product everywhere and, by so doing, build a company that would make my father proud. But after I thought of my father I realized that he might not be pleased about this project because he detested the idea of his children looking for contracts.

We arrived at our destination, a mighty skyscraper in the heart of Boston, at exactly 1:30pm, thirty minutes before our appointment. I was intimidated as I entered the building. My father was probably intimidated as well when he went to New York for the third part of his interview with the parent company of this same company. He had come all the way from Nigeria while I had come all the way from Virginia. I was trying to put myself in his shoes even though I knew that I did not have his courage.

We went up the elevator to the vice-president's office and were told by his secretary that we were early before she led us to the waiting room. My brother and I sat down, he noticed that I was very nervous. "You have to be bold and confident because no one will ever have confidence in someone who does not have confidence in himself."

In an effort to motivate me he went on to tell me a story about our father. He had wanted to impress his superiors, following his appointment as the controller of ITT in Nigeria, by making fervent efforts to retrieve a three million pound debt owed the company by the Nigerian ministry of defense. This debt had remained unpaid for over three years because a colonel responsible for payments of contracts opposed the settlement.

He was a powerful colonel, everyone was scared of him. He snubbed my father repeatedly and a quarrel broke out between the two of them. A powerful general, trying to settle the rift, asked my father if he knew who the colonel was. But my father responded by asking the general if the colonel knew who he was, even though he, my father, was just a company employee at that time. He took a big risk that could have gotten him arrested but it paid off because the colonel did not call his bluff but authorized payment that same day. "That is the kind of courage a businessman should have." concluded my brother. "Or else he would fail because fear can be as harmful as giving up from the beginning."

The secretary suddenly appeared and announced that it was time for us to see her boss then led us to his office. From the moment I saw the vice-president I knew that we were going to have a tough time with him. He was a tall man with brown hair and an elusive face. But what discouraged me the most was that I instantly had the feeling that he was a very conservative man, a man who resisted new ideas because he felt more comfortable implementing existing ones. He received us warmly, though, and politely asked that we get to the point.

My brother spoke first. Once again, he described our product in detail then I took over and highlighted the potential benefits of our product to his organization in detail, trying to establish a middle ground of interest at first before gradually shifting my focus to the gains of his organization, delivering what I considered to be a powerfully convincing pitch lasting almost five minutes. "But I don't see the logic in what you have said. You have not explained why we should do business with your company." The man seemed puzzled as his eyes bored on me. "We already have a working arrangement with a big telecom company that can easily offer your service so why should we do business with you?" His tone had become harsh which gave me the impression that he had ruled out the possibility of placing an order.

I was startled. This man either did not understand my presentation or wanted to ignore all that I had said. Or maybe I was speaking too fast and should repeat all that I had said. "Any big telecom company would have a range of core services, a category in which customized phone cards would certainly not belong." I was very anxious but my desperation surpassed my anxiety. "The prices that such a company would offer you cannot be competitive because customized phone cards are not profitable enough to be one of the core services of that kind of company with large overhead costs."

The words flowed out automatically. I gave him some time to absorb what I had said then quickly provided details of some special services offered by our service provider, without mentioning the company's name, to prevent the possibility of his company dealing directly with the service provider. I also made the strategic decision of reducing the price of each card to slightly above a dollar to serve as an additional incentive for him to place an order.

A pensive look appeared on his face for a few seconds then suddenly disappeared. Once again he stated his opposition to the idea but gave us a reason to be hopeful when he asked us to call him after five days. I was disappointed but slightly relieved that he had not rejected our proposal. We were about to leave but he had another idea. "Come with me, let's go and see the president upstairs. He will be thrilled because he is always going off about your father."

Chapter Seventeen

The president's office was a very short distance away. Once we reached there the vice-president rushed to inform him of our presence, leaving us with the president's secretary, a pleasant woman probably in her fifties. I finally met the woman to whom I had been talking and was almost tempted to ask her whether she had been responsible for the call that I had received from the other Sheraton official. I did not bother, though, because I was uncertain about what her reaction would be. The vice-president returned and led us to the door of his boss's office then said he was going back to his own office. I was amazed when I entered. I had never seen such a lovely office in my life. The furniture, rug and tables were all exquisitely unique and absolutely breath-taking.

The president spotted us and stood up to shake our hands. He was a short chubby man with distinctively piercing eyes. I did not remember meeting him before but my brother did. He urged us to sit close to him and feel at home. He acted as if he was more excited about the meeting than we were. He started talking about my father and, just like the vice-president had said, he did not want to stop. "One day he almost got us into trouble when he saw a fat woman and asked her when she was going to give birth." We all laughed. "But it wasn't his fault because he really thought that she was pregnant and tried to explain but she had already flared up."

"But how was he at work? How was he on the field?" I asked with a purpose in mind. "As a young businessman I wish he was around to reveal the secret of his success. I am lucky to see you because you know since you were there from the very beginning."

"Yes I was." He sounded more excited. "He was an amazing salesman. He hardly ever rested and his contributions helped to uplift the company in so many ways. He was so hard working, so persistent and he was always on the phone, trying to get things done."

My mother would have loved to hear such things about my father from a former expatriate because she had once told me that a lot of the expatriate staff disliked him for emphasizing on training Nigerian indigenous engineers on equipment maintenance. Expatriate engineers feared that they would become redundant as a result of what he was doing.

"I wish I had my father's marketing skills and extraordinary drive." I stated soberly. "I don't think that our meeting with the vice-president went as well as we had hoped." I added, looking for an avenue to market our products to the president directly.

He asked me to be optimistic and changed the topic to my father's present ordeal. "I have tried all channels to reach him but no luck. How is he doing?"

"Your guess is as good as ours because we don't have a clue." replied my brother then gave him details about how we had been prevented from seeing our father after our mother's death.

"I heard about her death." declared our host before adding. "And I am very sorry about that unfortunate incident."

"We named this company after her." I quickly muttered, knowing that our meeting would soon come to an end, determined to get him on our side. "Each card costs slightly over a dollar which is a very inexpensive and valuable gift to customers spending hundreds of dollars per night."

He smiled and assured us that our proposal would be seriously considered. "But why did my friend get involved in such a gamble? Wasn't he afraid of jail?"

I was silent briefly, for I did not know how to tell him that his friend was already in an emotional form of incaceration before his arrest following the cancellation of his electoral victory. My mother had entered his room several times and found him staring blankly at the ceiling as if his life was about to come to an end. I assured the president that he had nothing to worry about in the long run, "In Africa the road to power passes through a prison. Mandela and so many others were travelers on that same road and ended up becoming presidents." My remark brightened his mood once again and he became even more jovial than before.

After that we spoke about other issues and our meeting came to a beautiful end when he assured us once again that his company would consider our product. We escorted him to an office on another floor then exited the building. "I love Boston." I screamed after we had walked far away from the Sheraton building.

"You are the same person who described the weather here as every African's nightmare a few hours ago." teased my brother. "You are now talking from the other side of your mouth."

We both laughed then walked to the car and drove to where we were staying. I was in very high spirits on the way, for the president had proven that he was one of my father's few loyal friends. He had not yet awarded us a contract but his warm reception was priceless. Many other of my father's so-called friends had never deemed it fit to pay us a visit or call after our mother's death. Even I had seen my own fair share of fake friends, people who suddenly disappeared after my father was arrested.

My brother and I decided to spend one more night in Boston. We arrived at the woman's apartment shortly before 4pm. "There you are! I was just about to pick up the phone and inform 911 about two missing African males." She joked before adding, "Didn't your meeting begin at 10am?"

"I hope that you planned calling 911 from a public phone because the informant becomes the prime suspect in the absence of any lead." I stated cheerfully before responding to her question. "We had a second meeting after the first one."

I told her everything that happened from the moment we stepped out of her apartment. Many people in Nigeria believe that revealing good news, like I was doing, brings bad luck. I don't think so and continued talking as she listened attentively. "Such things can only happen in Boston and I hope you now know that." declared my hostess as a mocking smile lit her beautiful face. "And that is another reason why most Francophone people love being here."

Chapter Eighteen

The following day

Almost two days had passed before I returned to Virginia. I went to New York the next day to visit my friends and the woman whom I wanted to marry. One of the highlights of my trip was meeting a very interesting man described by my friend, his nephew, as one of my father's biggest fans. The man wanted to take me out for diner and I agreed a day before I returned to Virginia.

Before the conversation began I had a feeling that my father would dominate a large part of it but I was wrong because he actually ended up dominating the whole of it. "How old were you when you first realized that your father was such a powerful businessman?" asked the stout and bald man sitting right next to me while his nephew lit a cigarette.

His question was normal but his tone made him sound like a journalist. "Am I being secretly recorded?" I asked my friend, trying to sound like I was joking even though I was serious.

His uncle burst out laughing then stood up, bringing out all the contents in his pocket- a wallet and a set of keys- before stating. "My nephew might have told you that I used to be a journalist but that was ages ago." He sat down again. "I am now just an old man who wants to know more about a man he loves from his son. By the way, I love your mother as well."

I became more relaxed after he had said that. "I never knew that my father was such a powerful businessman until I was around ten years old when he began asking me and my siblings to help him tidy up his room." The man looked puzzled and I knew why. "He had a lot of domestic staff capable of cleaning his room but things were always getting missing and his children, according to him, were less likely to steal from him. In those days he spent hours on the phone, talking to his managers about his airline, his farms, his bakeries, his newspapers and his shipping company. I used to be startled because I had no clue of his massive wealth prior to that. My mother hardly spoke about it, for she wanted to bring up her children to be hard working and independent-minded."

"What did you like the most about him?" He asked eagerly, swiftly adding. "And which of his qualities did you dislike the most?"

"His generosity was very admirable and, sadly, the reason behind his current travails. I would never have believed that a man could have been as generous as him had I not been a direct witness to a particular incident." I paused then proceeded. "One day a stranger was ushered into his living room when I was arranging some of his documents for him. The stranger, a skinny looking man with a bald head, greeted my father then told him that his wife, who was about to be discharged from the hospital after giving birth, would come out to find herself homeless because his landlord had asked him to vacate his apartment immediately for not paying his rent on time." I paused again. "My father told the man, who had started crying by then, that the only reason why he was crying was because he was not yet aware of the fact that he was about to own a house. That same day he gave the man a house and instructed his lawyer to ensure that the property bears the man's name.

"What an amazing thing to do!" exclaimed the man, adding. "I have heard many similar stories about your father. Is it true that an Islamic cleric once told him that giving his wealth away would make it multiply?"

"And you believe that?" I burst out laughing then added. "But on a more serious note, my father has always believed that anyone who is unwilling to share things with others does not deserve to own anything.

"And his faults?" asked the man, suddenly sounding more like a detective.

"Women, women and women. He had a strong weakness toward the opposite sex, a weakness whose absence would have made him a much better person." There was a brief pause. "Another shortcoming that he had was his slight disregard for his personal family when waging this kind of battle against such evil forces. He owes more to his family, as a father and husband, than to any other segment of society."

The meeting lasted for two more hours during which we spoke about my father's soccer club and his childhood then they drove me back to my hotel and left. I went up to my room and thought that I would sleep right away but could not. After all that talk about my father I could not stop thinking about him and my mother. And as usual, whenever I got into such a pensive mood at night, my mind always drifted toward the negative side of things. Why did my mother stand in front of a moving train? Why had she not thought about the fate of her seven children in her absence? Why are Nigerians not revolting against the military ruler who arrested their president after stealing his presidency? I asked myself many other questions which compounded my depression. That night I was stunned by my mood swing and found it very hard to believe that I had been happy just a few hours ago.

My mother was not always a happy woman even before our political crisis, I reminded myself, as I felt some anger toward my father. I began having flashbacks of her complaints to me about her marriage even when I was very young. In those days we stayed at my grandmother's house whenever problems arose between her and my father. Then my thoughts shifted suddenly to my father as I wondered where he was that night. He was probably in a remote house somewhere surrounded by soldiers and other armed personnel who were meant to be subservient to him as the legitimate president of the Federal Republic of Nigeria.

Thinking about his helplessness reminded me of his charities to international organizations. I became furious that these organizations were not doing enough to help him. Had he not been a friend indeed? Was he not a friend in need? What is the use of all the awards given to him around the world if those who gave the awards were not speaking out for him now? He was the recipient of the symbolic key to Washington D.C., a key that was made of gold. He had been given an award from the prestigious National Association for the Advancement of Colored People. He had been honored with over two hundred Nigerian chieftancy titles by different communities in most parts of Nigeria. He was Africa's pillar of sports. The list was endless but all that meant nothing now because he had been abandoned.

Chapter Nineteen

The following day

It was time to call the vice-president. My brother agreed that I could make the call when I offered but I began regretting making that offer when it was time to dial the man's number. I had just returned to Virginia but was not tired at all. The hardest thing was figuring out the right time to call because I knew the importance of timing but, unfortunately, did not know the vice-president well enough to know his schedule.

I postponed calling him until after a short walk. The time was 11am. I would call the man at 12 noon, I told my brother, as I walked out of the house, strolling all the way to a shopping complex in Arlington Virginia. I returned fifty minutes later and was ready for the vice-president. I dialed his number after ten minutes and it rang for a while until he suddenly answered. He sounded more pleasant on the phone than in real life but he had bad news. "We are not interested because the product is not suitable for our chain of hotels." His tone was mild and polite, his words blunt and hurtful.

I listened carefully, my heart pounding out of grief. But I was not ready to take no for an answer. I was determined to make him change his mind, for my father has always said that anyone who tries and fails did not try hard enough. "Sir, I don't want to sound proud but watching you let this opportunity slip right through your fingers is not something that I want to happen, it is not something that I want on my conscience." My tone was aggressive because I was trying desperately to hold onto a dream that was about to slip away. "Customized phone cards with your logo are the best souvenirs that you can give to departing guests because most of them are travelers." I was not sure about that statistic. "With your cards they can call their families and friends if they are stuck at the airport because of bad weather or rescheduled flights. I can assure you that our product will place Sheraton above all competition because no other hotel is thinking this far ahead. No other hotel is offering such preciously inexpensive gifts to worthy customers." I paused. "By spending just over a dollar on a customer who has spent over a hundred dollars per night, you can prove that Sheraton cares about its customers beyond their stay at its hotels. You can prove that Sheraton is considerate."

My father had taught me that being considerate to customers is a very powerful tool in business. He knew this fact as a teenager and used it to make his musical band the best in the town he grew up by simply ensuring that his band members wore colors that reflected the mood of the event in which they performed (dark colors for funerals and bright ones for festive occasions), something that had been overlooked by other bands whose members wore the same colors to all events without regard to the nature of the event. He had not had any prior experience in music but that single step made his band a huge success.

The vice-president paused, I knew he was thinking about what I had said, and finally gave me a reason to remain optimistic. "Maybe your product can be useful in our luxury collection chain. You should get in touch with the man in charge of that department." suggested the vice-president before telling me the man's name and giving me his number then he hung up.

I began moving around the living room as my brother stared at me with a smile on his face. I had wanted to call the second man immediately but decided to give the vice-president enough time to inform him of my call. I spoke to him after an hour and was surprised that he seemed more excited about the product than me. "That is an excellent way of recognizing existing guests. Give me some time and I would come up with an ideal location to do a test run!"

He called me later and gave me the details of the location. He told me to fax him a quotation and, after a few days, he placed an order. The contract was executed successfully and our company was referred to others by the Sheraton Luxury Collection.

It was during that same period that my siblings and I were finally given an interview date for our political asylum application. We had applied from Virginia because that was where my brother, my mother's eldest child, was living when we applied.

We were all scared on our way to the interview because of the fear of rejection and being forced to return to Nigeria. I knew that our application would likely be approved but refused to focus on that fact because being overconfident about anything had always brought me bad luck. We hardly spoke to each other on the way. Even my two younger brothers, who were usually playful, looked very humorless.

We got to the venue and did not wait for long before we were called for our interview. The interviewer was very polite and asked us to sit down with a big smile which put me at ease. He looked at our file and asked a few questions. I wanted to show him some additional articles supporting our application but changed my mind because the man already seemed convinced about our eligibility for asylum. He smiled and told us that we would hear from his office soon then added, "You are all free to go."

That was it. The interview was over in less than five minutes. So all that fear and apprehension was for nothing. The fact that we were allowed to go technically meant that we had been granted asylum because I had heard stories about rejected people been whiskered away from their interviews then deported. I was not sure if those tales were actual facts or rumors and was not interested in finding out.

On our way home we discussed what would have happened if our application had been rejected. My youngest brother, Hadi, said he would have gone into hiding but I reminded him that he and his immediate elder brother had nothing to fear because their visas had not yet expired, "It is we, the older ones, who would be thrown out of the United States and sent back to Nigeria."

But he screamed. "Then who will take care of us if you guys are booted out?"

His remark was food for thought. We all laughed then cracked more jokes on our way home. I was thrilled that I could stay in a country as great as the United States for as long as I wished. I finally understood what people meant when they said that one never knows what one has until it is gone, for I began appreciating the United States more after experiencing the fear of being kicked out. That day was one of the best days in my life.

Chapter Twenty

My life was taking shape in the United States as the situation in Nigeria was further detoriating. A former military vice-president turned politician named Shehu Yar'adua died in jail. He had been injected with poison according to unconfirmed reports following a detention lasting several years for his alleged involvement in a failed coup against the government. He had been sentenced to death along with his former boss, a general and former military head of state named Olusegun Obasanjo. But General Abacha had spared their lives, however, when he bowed to international pressure and commuted their sentences to life imprisonment.

The harsh manner with which General Abacha had treated his two former military bosses was a clear indication of an increasing level of ruthlessness that triggered additional fears about my father. Prior to the general's actions army generals in power had always respected their seniors even after retirement as a form of esprit de corps. Then there was another unexpected development.

General Abacha accused his very loyal second-in-command General Diya of planning a coup, an indication of a growing paranoia that made him distrust almost everyone, forcing him to sleep in different places in the presidential palace to avoid assassination, spying on loyalists and setting traps for them. He wanted his second-in-command to serve as a lesson to others and, as a result, he spread a recording in which the man knelt on the floor and begged him for mercy in tears while he, General Abacha, sat on a chair and continued giving him a bunch of tissue papers to dry his tears.

The military ruler, meanwhile, had made up his mind to make his presidential ambition less elusive and set the ball rolling in different directions. Things began happening at an alarmingly accelerated pace by 1997 because of his plan to realize his ambition by either August or October of 1998 through a democratic contest in which he would be a sole candidate.

All the five registered political parties, funded by him and run by his stooges, would adopt him with the backing of a clause inserted in a new constitution that had not yet been made public, a new constitution for which there had not even been a referendum like the constitutions of some other African countries governed by similarly autocratic rulers.

"No wonder that idiot had my mother killed. She would have gone ballistic in reaction to all this madness." I was with a Nigerian political activist also living in the United States.

"But there is hope because opposition against him is mounting, even from the north where he comes from." stated the man in an effort to brighten my mood. "Recently more than a hundred northern university lecturers condemned his presidential ambition in a joint letter and warned that it was contrary to his earlier pledge of not contesting. At long last, Nigerians from all parts of the country are forming a united front against him."

I disagreed. "That is not true because every two people condemning him end up confronting two hundred people supporting him. This game is a game of money and money brings the numbers. That murderer has bought almost eighty percent of Nigeria's elite." He wanted to respond but I did not give him a chance. "Recently over sixty kings from all over the country paid him a royal visit and begged him to contest the presidential elections, they literally begged him, claiming that they were representing their subjects, then issued a joint statement in which they declared that no other Nigerian has the general's credentials. I have not even mentioned prominent politicians from all parts of the country who have adopted the 'No Abacha No Nigeria' slogan."

"But you ought to know that this kind of support is not genuine, it is a product of manipulation through money or force. Do you know that party officials opposed to the adoption of General abacha are whiskered away from the convention by armed personnel? It is as if you deliberately want to focus on negative things in order to protect yourself from being disappointed." Was he right about his last statement? Was that what I was doing? He continued talking. "Recently the G8 Summit, Susan Rice, the British foreign affairs minister and many others rejected Abacha's plan to be the sole candidate in the elections and demanded that he conducts a free and fair election involving other contenders to mark the end of his transition program."

He was dead wrong if he believed that his last comment would uplift my mood. "Why should we reinvent the wheel? Why should we cook a meal that is already cooked? Nigeria already has an elected president but yet, instead of demanding the release and installation of the legitimate president, they want a maniac like Abacha to conduct a free and fair election."

That same year the government announced a date for the registration of voters. The day came and, to my surprise, the event turned out to be a major flop despite the huge sums of money earmarked for the mobilization of rented crowds. But, as usual, there was a distorted official version of the outcome. Government officials described the event with words such as 'impressive' and 'beautiful'. One of them, an illiterate minister, stated that the turnout was astronomically astronomical. The man, rumored to be fond of sleeping with women in his office in exchange for contracts, probably did not know the meaning of those words because his English is as poor as his ethics.

Chapter Twenty-One

"There is order. People go about pursuing their legitimate interests. Then, what is the problem?"

General Abacha was talking in an interview, something that he hardly did‹ and was not making any sense as usual because the order of which he boasted was a figment of his own imagination. Disorder caused by members of his household, for instance, had become the talk of the town. One of his children had supposedly become the first daughter of any African dictator to have a letter heading carrying the words 'The Office of The First Daughter'. His children instructed ministers to 'rehabilitate' their friends, a term used by them for awarding contracts and his eldest son was alleged to have slapped the governor of the Central Bank for refusing to execute a particular directive. He also took pleasure in torturing political prisoners.

But such acts meant nothing to supporters of General Abacha who disregarded them and produced advertisements, sponsored by the government, such as a particular one hinting that Nigerians were lucky because they had gotten two leaders, the general and his wife, for the price of one. Another form of disorder during that period was evident in the quality of petrol sold in Nigeria. Abacha empowered a tiny clique of cronies to import petrol for the entire country after the refineries had collapsed and these people, with the aim of maximizing their profit, imported cheap adulterated petrol that destroyed many engines and polluted the air. That was the reason behind the foul smell that spread around major cities in Nigeria during that period.

The rest of the interview also reflected the wide gap between the Nigerian ruler and reality. "One reason we had to delay the local government election is because, in reports we received, these same people were planning to go to various polling centers and start bombing innocent people. People like Wole Soyinka, they are terrorists." declared the general as he falsely accused Nigeria's only Nobel Prize Laureate Wole Soyinka of terrorism.

Fifteen activists, also unjustly labeled as terrorists, were dragged to court three days before the government's controversial local government elections. They were accused of being the masterminds of various bomb blasts. One of them had been charged with the others simply because his name resembled a name that was found in the diary of a bomb blast victim.

There were also bloody clashes between protesters supporting the general and protesters opposing him which ended with many casualties and arrests. Those apprehended were charged for treason, locked up and, in what had become a pattern, brought to court in chains on their legs and handcuffs on their wrists. All these incidents contradicted the order that General Abacha was blabbering about.

The interview sparked an interesting discussion about dictators between me and a very intelligent American friend. "Do you think a dictator values his life more than power?" asked my friend at the beginning of our conversation.

"Power is definitely more important to them than their lives." I quickly replied, adding. "If you point a gun at a rich man and ask him to choose between his money or his life, he would likely choose his life but try asking a dictator with a gun in your hand to choose between power or his life and watch him try to grab the gun from you."

My friend laughed. "Don't you think you are exaggerating? Prove your point with an example!"

"Have you heard of Samuel Doe?" He shook his head then I continued. "He was a Liberian ruler who clinged to power despite the superior power of the rebels seeking his overthrow. He knew that his life was in danger but vowed to stay in power until the end. He was eventually killed like an animal after some parts of his body were cut off."

My friend paused for a while then arrived at the point he was trying to make. "If you know that dictators love power to that extent then your father, being a wiser man than you, should have been aware of that fact as well." He paused briefly. "Why didn't he use force since that is the only language that dictators like General Abacha understand? People who would rather be killed than give up power."

His question had been on my mind since my mother's death. "My father was advised by many people to follow that path but he disagreed and I respect him for that." I was being sincere but did not always feel that way. "Force is capable of producing the desirable results but at what price? How many innocent lives would be lost? Have you forgotten the saying that 'killing one person is like killing the whole world?' I believe in that saying." I paused briefly before concluding. "The ends must never be seen to justify the means in such matters because knowing where to draw the line becomes impossible when we see things that way. That is what dictators like Abacha fail to understand and that is how they transformed from humans with a conscience into animals without one."

Chapter Twenty-Two

February 1998

A former second-in-command with chains on his legs and handcuffs on his wrists was not an image that Nigerians expected to see on February 1998 when the military ruler's former deputy General Diya was brought to a military court. The man hopped when moving forward to avoid falling, serving as a warning to everyone that such humiliation would be the fate of anyone opposing General Abacha.

I did not believe that General Diya, whom I had once met personally, could have been involved in coup plotting. That was not the style of a lawyer turned soldier like him who was more refined than his boss. General Diya's major fault, I assumed, was the occasional inclination of people like him to make careless and harmless remarks about their superiors in the presence of moles, remarks that might have been overlooked during a normal period, but certainly not when the military ruler wanted to instill fear in the hearts of everyone in preparation for his transformation into a civilian president within eight months.

This trial reminded me of the first time that I heard of General Diya. It was a night in 1994. My father had come to the United States on that night and I had gone to Boston from New York to spend time with him. He was very jovial and went to sleep after a heavy diner and lengthy conversation with me and some of his other guests.

But a few hours later, almost at midnight, I heard a faint knock on my door. I opened my eyes and my father had opened the door and put on the light before I sat on my bed. He was gloomy. "Are you alright sir?" My voice was trembling. "Do you need anything?"

He sat on my bed before I could get up. "I remembered something that I want to forget." He paused then spoke again before I could say anything. "I remembered how General Abacha and Diya deceived me."

I knew how General Abacha had deceived him, my mother had told me the story, but who was Diya? I was studying in the United States then and did not know that he was General Abacha's deputy. "Who is the second person?" By then I had already forgotten his name, I have never been good with names.

My father laughed bitterly. "Oh, you mean Diya? We will get to his own part of the story but don't you want to know what happened from the beginning?"

I nodded my head, I wanted to hear everything even though I already knew some of what happened. By then I was wide awake but slightly worried about being able to wake up for my morning flight. "Abacha knew that the courts would rule against the interim government put in place following the annulment of my election because it was an illegal government. He reached out to me to prevent me from declaring myself as the president after such a ruling, assuring me of his support and promising to help me actualize my mandate if the interim government is sacked by the courts."

"And you believed him?" I spoke softly, for I did not want him to get offended by my question.

"What choice did I have? The army could have killed me if I had declared myself as the president then." snapped my father defensively, making me wish that I had phrased my question another way. "And the only reason that I am contemplating declaring myself the president now is that I am certain that there is no other way for me to become president."

"But if they could have killed you then they can still kill you now." The thought of losing him was terrifying.

"Am I not dead already?" His response was quick then he patted me on the shoulder, probably realizing that he should not have said that, before gently adding, "Don't worry, things will end well." He paused then continued his narrative. "The court eventually ruled against the interim government, as I had expected, and Abacha made contact with me, as I had hoped, but he introduced a strange twist to the matter." He paused with anger in his eyes. "He asked me to draft a strategy stating how the army could install me as the president. Can you imagine that kind of request coming from him out of all people?"

I was confused. "Him out of all people? I don't know what you mean by that, sir."

My father frowned, he seemed irritated by my question. "You would have understood If you were older in the 1980s. You see, Abacha might be a stack illiterate but he deserves a Phd in matters relating to coups. His expertise in this area accorded him the privilege of being the one to announce every military coup despite his terrible English." My father stood up, moving farther away from me and sitting on a chair next to my bed. "His request for a strategy was insincere because he knew how the army could have installed me as president. The first step would have been to summon the head of the dissolved National Electoral Commission and instruct him to announce the remaining unreleased results confirming my electoral victory. Then a judge would have sworn me in as the president. That is all but Abacha was pretending. He wanted to buy time to consolidate his plot of grabbing power for himself after the dissolution of the illegal interim government."

He stood up and shifted our discussion to General Diya. "I went ahead and drafted a strategy as he had requested. I knew that I was being naive but I did not want him to claim that I had frustrated his plan to install me as the president. But when it was time to deliver the strategy to him, he asked me to hand it over to General Diya, which I did. General Abacha later took over power, banned all political activities and sacked all civilian governors. He told me that I should have given Diya the written strategy during my first visit to him after he had assumed power. I told him that I had given it to Diya but he denied receiving it. I met Diya to demand an explanation but he said that he had given it to Abacha, marking the beginning of a game of hide-and-seek until Abacha was able to consolidated his power. I should have declared myself as president once the court had toppled the interim government."

That was less than four years ago and General Diya would have realized by now that he should have been dining with the devil with a much longer spoon. But his courage in court impressed me. He was very bold as he described himself as a victim of a plot orchestrated from the very top. It was hard to believe that he was the same man who had begged General Abacha in tears, and on his knees, in a widely publicized recording.

One thing I could not understand then, and still cannot comprehend now, was how an intelligent man like him would have ever agreed to work for a man like Abacha. If money had been his motivation then his recent predicament would have made him realize that it should never have been.

Chapter Twenty-Three

A month later

Nigerians had a real reason to rejoice, at least I did. Pope John Paul 11 was going to Nigeria on a three-day visit. I have never been a Christian but that did not stop me from rejoicing because I regarded his visit as a form of divine intervention. His earlier trip to Cuba that same year had been accompanied by the immediate release of over two hundred and ninety political prisoners.

I was certain that the pope would want to help my father because, despite being a Muslim, my father had built a lot of churches in Nigeria. His bond with Christianity dated back to his early days at a secondary school named Baptist Boys' High School, established by the American Southern Baptist Convention.

I became curios about the pope, I wanted to find out everything about him in order to know what to expect or whether to expect anything. Pope John Paul 11, originally known as Karol Jozef Wojtlya, was born in Poland on May 18, 1920 and was the first non-Italian pope in the Vatican's history. I read many details about his steady rise in the Vatican until he attained his current exalted position.

But I became less optimistic about his trip after a brief chat with a friend. "Don't get your hopes high about the pope's visit because your father is not one of the Catholics constituting ten percent of Nigeria's population." declared my cynical friend, adding, "I am sorry for being so blunt but you know that I always like telling you the truth."

"I know but this time you are wrong. This pope is different, everything about him is different. He is sincere and selfless." I sounded confident although I was no longer sure about what I was saying. "He even persuaded Fidel Castro to release hundreds of political prisoners. Do you know how hard he must have tried to get someone like Castro to - "

"Don't believe all you read in the papers because the more you look at these people the less you see." continued my friend stubbornly, interrupting me. "World leaders are not like you and me, they are in a world of their own with their own rules. By the time you investigate that Cuban incident deeply, you will find out that most of those prisoners were either Catholics or that their release served the interest of the Catholic Church one way or the other."

"You are a Christian but yet you are so eager to condemn the most powerful Christian leader. How can you be so suspicious of a man who breaks down walls that divide people? A man who has been pressurizing China to accept religious freedom, a man who fights against the death penalty, a man who promotes peace between Muslims and Christians and a man who has been of great help to disabled children."

He stared at me strangely and I became embarrassed because I had sounded like a Vatican spokesman. But what choice did I have? I was desperately clinging onto the hope that the pope would help secure my father's release. I changed the topic and never brought it up with him or anyone else. But a few days later, just before the pope's arrival, I heard that the main purpose of his trip was a particular event, the beautification ceremony of a deceased priest named Father Cyprian Iwene Tansi, a man who had passed away in a British monastery more than three decades ago. I was angry because I felt that, with all due respect to the dead, the pope should have also been going to Nigeria for other reasons. I became cynical and began thinking that my friend might have been right in his assertions.

The pope finally came and impressed me by always talking about human rights and democracy in all the places he went. I was delighted because I assumed that he was sending a message to Nigeria's oppressive government. But he soon shifted his attention to mediating between clashing religious groups, urging them to embrace harmony instead of acrimony. He met with Muslim leaders separately and surprised a lot of people by spending as much time with them as he did with their Catholic counterparts. The beautification ceremony also took place, as planned, and attracted at least one million people.

I became impatient to hear about his efforts toward political prisoners, however, as the trip came closer to an end but was frustrated because I only heard irrelevant rumors about his trip. There was talk of how a new house was built for him before his arrival because a pope is not allowed to sleep in a house formerly occupied by anyone, and that this new house would remain shut after his departure until another pope comes to Nigeria. There was also some uproar when General Abacha wore a completely black outfit to receive the pope.

I almost lost hope in the visit, though, when a minister- a day before the pope's departure- stated that the pope's presence in Nigeria was proof of the country's stability. The pope had not been exerting enough pressure on the military government to free detainees, I concluded, but was relieved when I heard that he had requested for the release of sixty political prisoners in a list that included my father's name.

General Abacha remained silent about this request during the remainder of the pope's visit. Many people assumed that he had either forgotten about the request or was just trying to display a form of disrespect toward the pope for meddling into Nigeria's affairs. But one day, after the pope had gone, a miracle happened. The military ruler suddenly decided to set some political prisoners free, something that he had not done in a long time. I was elated when I heard the news and hoped that my father would be one of them. But that did not happen, turning the hope that accompanied the pope's visit into despair.

Chapter Twenty-Four

That same period

My father was gradually fading into the past which put me in a permanent state of anxiety coupled with depression surrounded by suspense and apprehension. But was he dead or alive? Once in a while, out of frustration, I wanted to hear that he was dead in order for the pain to worsen then hopefully lessen. After all I would be forced to accept the reality and move on with my life.

I wanted to see a counselor in those days, a normal thing for anyone suffering from emotional problems to do, but changed my mind because such an action is regarded as a taboo in Nigeria where counselors are only meant to attend to the mentally deranged. I thus embraced religion, a practice common among Nigerians facing unbearable emotional pain, and began spending more time in a mosque near my house. The mosque was not a walking distance from where I lived but I was determined to perform all my five daily prayers there.

During that period I met quite a number of Nigerian diplomats stationed at the embassy in Washington D.C. The majority of them were Muslim Northern Nigerians like General Abacha and I valued their company because, since they did not know who I was, they were a valuable source of vital information. One of them, though, became a good friend. We used to meet outside the mosque and got along very well until he made a comment one day that sparked a major conflict between us. "These southerners are foolish. They want to take the law into their own hands as if the law cannot twist their hands and break them." declared my northern friend in condemnation of a rally organized by the United Action for Democracy, a group in Nigeria that was still bold enough to oppose the military ruler's plans of becoming a civilian president. "Why are you quiet? I hope that you are not in support of the actions of these Yoruba hooligans." continued the man as if he had forgotten that I was a southerner from the Yoruba tribe that he had just insulted.

This same man had complained of being a victim of the system opposed by this group that he was condemning. He had once confided in me that, unlike the children of some northern elites in the government, he worked five times as hard to attain his mediocre position in the ministry of foreign affairs. So why was he now defending a regime that he had accused of keeping a few people on top at the expense of a majority at the bottom destined to a life of perpetual penury?

For the first time one of the junta's most prominent members, a military state administrator named Ahmed Usman, declared that protesters will henceforth be considered as prisoners of war in reaction to violent rallies that had taken place in the state he governed. People lost their lives and their properties were destroyed. But such sacrifices meant nothing to the man in front of me.

"Those foolish southerners want a change that will bring about relief to your own people in the north. Those foolish southerners are risking their lives for themselves and, of course, for your own people." I paused, fuming in rage. "Maybe that is why they are foolish or can there possibly be another reason?" He looked perplexed and did not answer which encouraged me to continue. "Have you forgotten that you once told me that General Abacha preserves a system that is detrimental to the interest of the northern poor, a system favoring a tiny cabal that has put Northern Nigeria in the list of the world's poorest regions?"

He paused for a while before responding. "You might be quoting me out of context and I don't blame you. I talk carelessly sometimes after a bad day at work but most things that I say at such occasions should not be taken seriously." He paused briefly. "Don't get me wrong, I am not saying that General Abacha does not have any shortcomings, he has many of them, but that does not erase the fact that we are indebted to him for unifying Nigeria when Abiola tried to divide it simply because he wanted to rule."

I could not believe my ears. Where did that come from? Did he really say what I had just heard? Had this man lost his mind or was he drunk? I became outraged and quickly looked around the mosque and saw a lot of people. I decided to get him away from the crowd and suggested that we take a walk and return when it was time for prayers. He agreed.

Once we were outside, I led him to a spot with a bench near the parking lot but preferred that we remained standing. "Do you remember that you once told me that Abiola helped the northern poor even more than most of their elites did?" He nodded, I continued. "Do you remember that Abiola won the elections in the northern and southern part of the country despite the fact that his vice-presidential candidate was a Muslim just like him?" Once again he nodded then I asked my third and most important question. "In that case, how can you say that a man who united Nigerians by making them forget their tribal and religious differences for the first time in their history was trying to divide Nigeria? How can you say something that stupid?"

He was startled by my anger and did not reply for a long time. "Why are you taking this matter so personally? We are just having a discussion.

Do you have something against me because I am from the north? Or have I offended you without realizing it?"

People had begun staring at us but I was not bothered. "I have nothing against you and you have never offended me but you will if you delay answering my question."

Chapter Twenty-Five

The man responded after almost a minute, speaking with a faint voice as if he had been asked to solve a mathematical equation. "Abiola did not want to divide the country, I should not have put things that way. What I ought to have said was that the people around him were the ones who wanted to divide the country." He paused briefly. "I am referring to the Yoruba nationalists, members of his own tribe, who have hijacked his electoral victory and turned it into a southern initiative. They want to split Nigeria and need him to achieve their selfish aim. Abiola is an excellent man but he should never have allowed the likes of such people to tarnish his image."

This was not the first time that I was hearing this propaganda. It was part of the military plot to discredit my father after the annulment of the election. His enemies spread rumors in the north that he was going to sell the northern part of the country to the United States and he was not spared in the eastern part of Nigeria as well where rumors circulated that he had caused a ship loaded with bibles to sink in the high sea. Most people in that region are Christians.

The propaganda had worked because this man seemed convinced about his statements. There was no point talking to him any longer. I turned around and walked away but had barely taken a few steps when I heard his voice right behind me. "Where are you going? Don't let politics spoil our friendship or have you forgotten that, as brothers in Islam, we should not let the devil come in between us?" He held my hand and stopped me from moving forward. "Do you know Chief Abiola?"

Once again he had surprised me. My father whom he had called 'Abiola' recklessly had now become 'Chief Abiola' because he now sensed that I was someone who valued him. "Yes I know him. He is my father and my mother is Mrs. Kudirat Abiola."

All of a sudden the man froze for a few seconds then all sorts of expressions appeared on his face as a result of his confused and embarrassed state of mind. He was regretful, startled, ashamed and flabbergasted. Looking at him, I got the feeling that he wished he could erase all he had said from my memory. Then, sounding like a patient cured from Alzheimer's disease, he began recalling details from the past in an agitated tone. "Oh my God, what a lovely surprise!" He paused then continued. "I was lucky to have seen your father once, what a humble man! He mixed with the poor as if he is one of us. That was when he came to Kano to campaign for the elections." He paused again. "By the way that is where I am from. Did I ever tell you?" He did not wait for an answer. "The people went crazy. Why wouldn't they go crazy? They loved him and still do. There can only be one Chief Abiooolaaaa." He had pronounced my father's name as if it were a song. "Kano is where his opponent is from but your father won there as well. He gave the man a solid trashing." After that he became more personal. "You have his eyes but your mother's nose." I thought it was the other way around. "Her killers will never know peace. They will perish. They will die a miserable death. Then they will be thrown into a bottomless pit on the Day of Judgment and-"

"Amen.. Amen." I interrupted him. I wanted to tell him to shut up because I had heard enough and was still angry with him. But he continued talking, this time he apologized. "Please forgive me! I know that I should not have said what I said. It was the devil. You know the devil always plots but God is the best of planners."

I looked at him seriously for a while then began laughing because he looked and sounded like a clown. Besides, it has always been part of my nature to calm down quickly after getting angry. We took a short walk during which I told him the bitter truth.

I made it clear to him that he had made those earlier comments because he was being tribalistic, adding that tribalism and corruption are connected to each other and are jointly responsible for Africa's backwardness. "Let's assume that I am a minister and that you are competing for a position in my ministry against a less competent candidate but I decide to give the position to the other candidate simply because he is from my tribe, Who loses?" I continued because he did not reply. "The country loses, of course, because tribalism encourages incompetence and incompetence leads to corruption. That is the link between tribalism and corruption. Now can you imagine the outcome when the same scenario occurs in multiple places simultaneously? It becomes a monumental disaster." He wanted to say something but I had not yet finished. "Tribalism is what made you prefer having a greedy and visionless leader like Abacha to a man like my father even though, as you said, your people voted for him. And you justified your support for Abacha by brainwashing yourself to thinking that he unified the country even though he divided it by locking up Nigeria's popularly elected president."

By the time we had finished our discussion, he agreed that Nigeria must be rid of General Abacha and that my father's presidential mandate must be restored for the country to move forward. But I was not happy even though he was being sincere because persuading him had required so much effort. Tribalism is definitely a more powerful force than I had imagined.

On my way back home I decided to do a better job at controlling my temper henceforth and to allow people to think and say whatever they wanted about my father. After all no one is loved by everyone, not even Mahatma Gandhi. A Hindu nationalist shot him after his great service to India. There had even been prior attempts on his life. I felt better when I began seeing things that way. No one is loved by everyone.

Chapter Twenty-Six

June, 1998

All of a sudden, from the middle of nowhere, rumors that General Abacha was sick began gaining grounds. I did not believe them at first. Was there any truth behind them? Most people, including me, had no way of finding out. From the rumors tales came to life of how a bed-ridden General Abacha had begged religious clerics to come to his aid and of how those clerics had instructed him to do a number of bizarre things if he really wanted to remain healthy enough to rule Nigeria for many more years. They told him, for instance, to eat wild animals like lions to gain strength and to bury the uneaten parts of those animals around the presidential palace. Another instruction was for him to find a virgin above twenty-eight years old with whom he would sleep with only once. The list of their demands on the frail Abacha was long and the fact that these rumors were so strong and many people believed that he had carried out those directives turned him into a laughing stock.

One thing that became clear to me as General Abacha's health detoriated was that he was not in control of power but power was in control of him. This explained his strong reluctance to attend to his failing health abroad. His days were numbered once he placed the fear of a coup above his health. His life came to an abrupt end, sooner than expected, on June 8, 1998, four days after the anniversary of my mother's death and four days before the anniversary of my father's presidential election.

General Abacha, they say, died on that day from a Viagra overdose in the hands of some Indian prostitutes after eating a poisonous apple but I never investigated the exact circumstances of his death. I never bothered to find out, for I regarded his departure as very good riddance to very bad rubbish. Once General Abacha was out of the way, another General named Abdulsalam took his place. Nigeria's new ruler, who had been General Abacha's defense chief, gained some instant credibility once rumors began spreading that General Abacha was about to sack him before his death. I was happy to hear those rumors and immediately took a liking to the new ruler. It was a rational thing to do since he had fallen out with Abacha before his death and the enemy of my enemy deserves to be my friend.

I truly believed that the new ruler was different from Abacha but after a few days I realized that both men were birds of the same feather. The only difference between them is that General Abacha was openly wicked while Abdulsalam covered his cruelty with a mask of humility. Exactly a week after he became the military president, he released all political prisoners apart from my father. These political prisoners had been arrested after my father and yet they had been released before him. And most of them. ironically, enjoyed better health than my father whom, according to reliable sources, had been complaining in vain to his guards of having malaria and fever. His pleas were ignored.

That was not all. Abdulsalam did not allow my family members to see my father nor give him access to proper medical attention even though, as a former defense chief to the late General Abacha, he was certainly aware of his numerous health problems. He did not care because he wanted my father dead, I concluded, as I hoped and prayed for a miracle just like I had done when General Abacha was alive. I had tasted hope, thinking the worst was over after the death of the former ruler, but that hope was painfully turning into a mirage

Chapter Twenty-Seven

My father was being badly treated. In a leaked letter he described himself as a man who had been abandoned in an open grave. General Abdulsalam further proved his wickedness by exposing my father to an emotionally rigorous political exercise as if his health problems were not bad enough. The Nigerian ruler invited global topshots like the then Secretary General of the United Nations Kofi Anan and the then Secretary General of the Commonwealth Emeka Anyaoku to have meetings with my father before even allowing his own family members to see him.

I am sure that these top diplomats were not aware of this, for such principled men would never have allowed something like that to happen under their watch. My father, after being isolated for so long, had even believed that Boutros Ghali was still the Secretary General of the United Nations when he met Kofi Anan. The only positive development from these diplomatic visits was the certainty that my father was still alive.

The poor man must have been overwhelmed by these encounters portrayed by the military government as a means of finding a way out of the political logjam triggered by the annulment of his presidential election. But the government was not being sincere. It was just buying time and that was evident in its refusal to make any concessions. My father, meanwhile, held onto his presidential mandate which, I strongly suspect, was why the new military ruler decided to eliminate him.

Then all of a sudden, thirty-three days after the death of General Abacha, Abdulsalam finally granted approval for members of my family to see my father. I was still in the United States then but my stepmothers, Mrs. Adebisi Abiola and Mrs. Doyin Abiola, and my father's eldest child, Lola Abiola, went to Abuja to see him and they did. They spent a long time with him and at long last he was able to see members of his family.

A few hours after that historic meeting, my father was summoned to another one. This time he was to meet the United States Undersecretary of State Thomas Pickering, Susan Rice and some American diplomats. My father was normal on the way to the meeting, according to the testimony of a police officer named Theodore Bethel Zadok, who declared in a statement that he had been responsible for my father's well-being in the last two years and that my father considered him as a son. But by the time they arrived at the venue, the government defense house known as Aguda House, he, Theodore Zadok, received a call on his radio instructing him to proceed to the office of the second-in-command of Nigeria's military government. He left my father with the Chief Security Officer of the military president after he had led him inside the venue of the meeting with the American government officials.

After Zadok returned within less than an hour he was informed by the chief security officer that my father had drunk a cup of tea and had fallen down. He rushed inside and saw my father lying on the floor. That was when he and two white men carried my father to a car and took him to the hospital of the military president where doctors battled in vain to save his life until he died after ninety minutes.

I got a phone call once news of his death spread around the world. I was watching a movie at home. The caller told me that my father had died. I did not believe him because he is not a Nigerian and I thought that he was confusing the name 'Abacha' with 'Abiola'. I added that Abacha had died more than a month ago but he remained adamant that it was my father whom he was referring to. I got angry with him and hung up.

Shortly afterwards I heard that President Bill Clinton also spoke of my father's death, announcing that he was certain that there was no foul play. That was when I realized that the worst had happened. Clinton's statement was later confirmed by an autopsy that stated that there was indeed no direct foul play. It stated that the cause of my father's death was most likely his heart that was described as 'diseased' by the autopsy report. Many people had doubts about this report and said that my father had drunk a cup of tea that contained poison given to him by the Americans.

I disregarded such claims and believed that they were sponsored by the military government to divert attention from General Abdulsalam. After all it was he who had refused to release my father for over a month after the death of General Abacha. He had allowed my family members to see him just a few hours before his death probably to serve as a cover-up for his assassination plan that was about to unfold. Even if I want to be less dramatic, the mere fact that General Abdulsalam denied my father of medical attention has made him liable for his death.

My father was buried in our house after his body was transported back to Lagos, marking the end of my fruitless wait to see him. I had wanted to tell him so many things. I had wanted to let him know that even if his stolen presidency was never recovered, his courage had made him greater than any other African president.

Once again, just like when my mother died, I could not attend my father's burial because I was still in the United States when he passed away. I felt like a foreigner as I watched the news of his death on CNN just like I had watched the news of my mother's death on CNN. The report was a long one. It covered his personal life, businesses and the tragedy that followed his death when some of his tribal kinsmen in Lagos killed more than fifty innocent people from northern Nigeria. It seemed like a nightmare and I had hoped it was.

After my father's death some sympathetic police officers leaked out some of his letters. I scrutinized each word in those letters, one after the other, because they were his final words. He spoke of his plan to visit Saudi Arabia to thank God for sparing his life. He spoke of his intention to revive his businesses that had been destroyed. He described the death of my mother as very painful, naming her the mother of his political struggle. But what surprised me the most was the letter he wrote to the wife of General Abacha in which he condoled her over her husband's death. I was shocked that he still had his forgiving spirit after the ordeal that he had been through.

Once my father was out of the way, General Abdulsalam, who had been evasive about his government's transition to civilian rule, finally announced that he would quit power in less than a year and that he would hand over to a democratically elected president. He also praised my father, saying that he was just about to release him then he prayed for his gentle soul to rest in peace. This reminded me of how General Abacha had also prayed for my mother after she had died even though he had sent his agents to kill her.

The Nigerian military finally left power on the May 29, 1999, less than a year after my father's death. In honor of my father, they chose their preferred presidential candidate from Ogun State, my father's state of origin. Since then the military has stayed away from governance and democracy has flourished in Nigeria, Africa's most populous country. That was how President Moshood Abiola, my father and the president who never ruled, and Kudirat Abiola, my mother and his most loyal supporter, won in death the battle that claimed both their lives during their search for the stolen presidency.

Epilogue

On July 20, 2001, Theodore Bethel Zadok testified at a panel named the Oputa Panel. He said that part of his job had been to drink or eat anything before it was given to my father and that he had not been able to do so on the day that my father died because he had been sent on an assignment. Toward the end of his testimony he directed three questions to the Chief Security Officer to General Abdulsam, the Nigerian military ruler at the time of my father's death: who gave Chief Abiola tea in my absence? Who tasted the tea before giving it to him? And in whose presence was the tea tasted?

Before that panel was formed, an army officer named Sergeant Rogers had confessed in court that he was the person who shot my mother. He declared that he was acting under the instructions of Major Al-Mustapha, the Chief Security Officer to General Abacha, the former military president and Mohammed Abacha, his son. Sergeant Rogers was in tears. Mohammed Abacha and around five other people were arrested, including one of my mother's close aides.

I was initially happy about those developments but I soon lost interest in them because I know the kind of country that I live in. Heroes are hardly recognized and justice is never delivered. Things are always swept under the carpet in the interest of powerful people with deep pockets. That was why I was not surprised when there was talk of a deal between the federal government and the Abacha family in which the Abachas would return almost a billion dollars in exchange for all charges against Mohammed Abacha being dropped. Mohammed Abacha was soon released even after his driver had admitted that Mohammed had sent him to drive the car from which my mother was shot and that Mohammed had given him money twice to flee to a neighboring country to escape interrogation over the murder. After Mohammed was freed, the Abachas reneged on their pledge to return money to the government. Another major development was the publication of a book written by Professor Humphrey Nwosu, the head of the National Electoral Commission during my father's election, in which he released the results of the polls and confirmed my father's victory.

I decided to begin ignoring news relating to those tragic events and move on with my life. My other siblings also adopted a similar approach. Out of my mother's seven children, only three of us (I, lekan and Mumini) permanently live in Nigeria where we all run our separate businesses, two petrol stations, a translation company, a construction firm and an IT company. My elder sister, Hafsat, partly lives in Belgium with her husband and Nigeria where she runs the Kudirat Initiative for Nigerian Democracy, a prosperous NGO specializing in the empowerment of women named after my mother.

My mother's remaining three children, Khafila, Moriam and Hadi remained in the United States where they have all become citizens. Khafila specializes in human resources, Moriam is a real estate consultant and Hadi, the youngest in the family, is an auditor.

I have never thought of going into politics although someone once almost talked me into it. It was on a special day in 2001. I had been given the prestigious title of the Shettima Rasheed of Borno which had been given to my father in the same state of Borno more than two decades before that day. It is a powerful title designated for the religious adviser to the king of Borno, known as the Shehu of Borno. My father had earned the title because he had sponsored many Islamic projects in Nigeria. Borno state is coincidentally where General Abacha came from.

I rode a horse for the first time in my life to the ceremony attended by governors and senators. The governor of the state made the state presidential lodge available to me to accommodate my family members and to receive my guests after the ceremony. It was one of those visitors who brought up the issue of politics. He was a learned cleric whom I had heard of prior to meeting him that evening for the first time. "Since we have elections every four years, we would have one in the year 2003, 2007, 2011, 2015, 2019 and 2023. How old will you be in 2023?" asked the cleric after a long conversation.

I was puzzled. "If I am alive, I will be forty-seven years old at the beginning of that year and forty-eight at the end of it."

He smiled warmly then said. "Your answer came swiftly. You have a sharp mind just like your father's mind." He paused then quickly added. "2023 will be exactly thirty years after the presidential election that your father won in 1993. That would be the perfect time for you to recover his mandate by running for office and winning.. You will win."

I burst out laughing. It took me a while to reply. The idea really excited me. "Do you really think I will win just like that?" I did not give him a chance to reply. "But what if I win and the presidency is stolen again? What if.."

He interrupted me. "How many times can a presidency be stolen in the same country from the same family?" He paused. "Don't be cynical! Yes, you will win just like that. Your father has already laid the foundation for you to be president tomorrow just as he laid the foundation for you to become the Shettima Rasheed of Borno today. Start planning now and just wait and see what will happen!"

I laughed again. Other people came to greet me and he excused himself to leave. I stood up and escorted him all the way to the gate of the presidential lodge. We exchanged numbers then I shook his hands and he left. I returned inside and attended to my other visitors but by the time I was ready to sleep, I was surprised to discover that I was no longer excited about the presidential idea. It was as if the man had gone with it the same way he had come with it.

Made in the USA
Columbia, SC
13 October 2023

24222819R00080